REAL TALK

No Bullsh*t Life Advice for Young Men

BY D.S.O.

www.dadstartingover.com

WHO THIS BOOK IS FOR

I wrote this book specifically for heterosexual teenage boys. You could be a young man in the early stages of puberty, or a guy that soon will be graduating high school. To be honest, many adult men will probably benefit from this book, too. This is, in no way, shape or form, a snub against our gay or bisexual brothers. Their experience is every bit as important and valid as us heterosexual dudes. I'm just drawing from my own experience as a straight dude who has lived the challenging and often confusing life as a teenage boy who was crazy about girls and confused about life.

If you're a hetero teen boy who is more than a little crazy about females right now, not sure about your role in life, and you want to be the kind of dude who has to beat girls away with a stick, this book is for you.

A NOTE TO PARENTS

If you are a parent that purchased this book for your teenage boy… thank you! I appreciate you putting your trust in me. I know it's not a small gesture. BUT, I want to get some things out of the way so that you are fully aware of what you are giving to your awesome young man.

1. **I do use foul language. Sometimes.** Not a lot. It's what I do when I write. Sometimes a good *"shit"* thrown here and there gets the job done. Trust me, your son has heard it all. It's not a big deal. He better get used to it now because he's going to hear a lot more of it as he gets older.

2. **I am pretty open and blunt about the topics of puberty and sex.** The time of \or talking *"carefully"* about sex is over. Your son is now a teenager. He needs this information to be blunt, honest, and to the point. Boys can sense when people are bullshitting them. This is a book that just tells it like it is. If that bothers you, or goes against your religious or moral sensibilities, then this book isn't for you. But, to be honest, he will get some of this information in one way or another. It might as well come from a forty-something-year-old author who has his best interests in mind and not some dumb fifteen-year-old friend who thinks he knows everything because he watched too much porn.

3. **Read through the book yourself.** Highlight stuff that you think may require some follow-up conversation. Don't be too pushy, especially about the sexual stuff. If something

rings true for you and you have a personal story to help push the point, please share that with your kid. Boys tend to love stories from their fathers about their own childhoods.

Thanks again for purchasing the book. Now, give this to your kid and let him get to work.

A LITTLE ABOUT ME AND THIS AWESOME BOOK

My real name is Ralph. Sorry, I wish it was something cooler. I usually go by the pen name *"DSO"* (which stands for *"Dad Starting Over"*) because I don't really need everyone in the world knowing who I am. I don't mind being anonymous. I'll leave the *"being kinda internet famous"* thing for the next guy. You won't ever see me flexing my G-Wagon on Instagram (I don't have a G-Wagon, by the way… I drive a seven-year-old Ford Explorer). I like my privacy. I'm a writer primarily because I enjoy peace and quiet.

I'm also old. Well, I'm not *"old"* by most people's standards, but by your standards… yeah, I'm old. I'm forty-seven. I have four kids. I've been married… twice. Still with the second wife, by the way. She's pretty amazing. Smart and sexy, if I do say so myself.

I'm an author of a few other books aimed at men having trouble with their marriages or lives after divorce. One of those books, *"The Dead Bedroom Fix,"* sold a lot of copies. It's aimed at men who aren't getting any sex from their wives. Yeah, it's a huge issue. Trust me. A lot of what I learned from writing that book and listening to my readers can be found in this book. It's just universal knowledge that we should all know, the earlier, the better.

In addition to authoring books, I also sell my time to guys who need my help coaching them through issues they have in their day-to-day life. One thing I've heard more than a few hundred times is something like, *"Man… why didn't they teach us this shit when we were kids?!"* After hearing that for the eight hundred forty-third time, it finally clicked: *"Maybe I should write a book about this for teenage boys."*

So, what you have in your hands right now, young man, is generations of wisdom that many of us had to learn the hard way. A rare few of us had a father figure tell us this stuff, but most of us didn't. Most of us had to get kicked in the balls by life a few times, and then we finally came to our senses. Sometimes that wasn't until after some pretty nasty stuff happened to us because we were blissfully ignorant our whole lives. I've heard some HORROR stories from dudes that made some big life mistakes. You don't want to go down that road. It's not pretty.

What I'm not going to do in this book is talk down to you. I'm not going to write this as if I was talking to a twelve-year-old. I'm going to write like I'm talking to a man… because that's precisely what you are. I'm going to treat you how I would want to be treated. That may mean that I say some big words here and there. If I think it may be a word you don't know, I will define it for you. Congrats, you just learned something new. That's what men do. Continuously. Until the day we die. We learn and we get better. You will find out that this is what the world expects of us.

This book will also be relatively short. It's not going to

be like a giant Stephen King novel. If there's one thing I've learned when writing over the years, it's that men like it when people just hurry up and get to the damn point. Men don't like a lot of fluff and nonsense. Young men, especially, don't have a lot of patience. Let's be honest, many of you have the attention span of a chihuahua on meth.

This book is something that could potentially be a real life-saver for you. I hope it's not too lame, and I hope you gain a few nuggets of wisdom that lead you to a fulfilling life as a man.

Now do all of us old dudes a favor. Read this book and put the words into practice. We want to watch you grow into the proud young man we wish we could've been.

INTRODUCTION –
YOU DON'T SUCK

I remember when I was around your age. Early teens. Oof... I would not do those years again. It was not fun.

I was what you would call an *"early bloomer."* Around eleven years of age, I started growing facial hair and sprouting body hair in several weird places (a phenomenon that continues well into my late forties). Then my voice started cracking. Then giant pimples grew on my forehead and back. The body odor could no longer be ignored. Multiple showers per day were needed. I was annoyed by everyone and everything around me. I was in a constant state of irritation.

This was my body's way of announcing to the world:

"I am becoming a man."

The biggest change of them all was one that wasn't so obvious to everyone around me. It wasn't the hair, pimples, body odor... no. It was the crazy mental state that I was in.

I was absolutely obsessed with girls.

My head was on a swivel. I was checking out EVERYTHING that resembled a human female. If it was an actual human, or just a picture in the Sears catalog (a pre-internet thing), or a fuzzy video image of a naked boob on Cinemax on the black-and-white TV in my bedroom late at night (another pre-internet thing)... I was looking at the female form with all the intensity of a hungry lion.

I couldn't get enough of girls.

My friends' moms suddenly went from being mother figures to, *"I wonder what she looks like naked."* My friends' older sisters went from being gross brats to girls that I would regularly fantasize about. My gym class went from being pumped about playing kickball to shamefully hiding my erection because Jennifer was wearing those tiny red shorts again.

The physical and mental changes were one thing, but my changes brought about something else that I wasn't prepared for: The way society would treat me.

As an early teen, most of my world revolved around school. You went to class all day... and at the end of the day, you participated in a sport or extra-curricular activity. All of these activities were usually associated with the school. Then you went home and did homework. Just another way for the school to further infiltrate your life. You probably had an hour or two a day at the end of the day, if you were lucky, that wasn't associated with the school in some way.

Therefore, my goal was to figure out how to navigate this world of my new changing teen body and my new changing teen mind within the framework of the almighty SCHOOL. After all, school took over about 95% of my waking life. This, I would learn, was not an easy task.

The school was well aware of us boys and the perfectly natural changes we were all going through. Much of the school curricula now seemed to be geared towards one thing: *"We gotta keep these boys in line, or else they will destroy everything."* They had a point. Young men CAN be destructive. Let's be honest. You've probably had more than one friend that said, *"Dude, watch this,"* as he did something EXTREMELY stupid that ended in destroyed property, skin lacerations, and/or broken bones.

However, what the schools did wrong was a common thing: They took things juuuuust a bit too far. We ended up with a bunch of boys who felt even weirder and more shameful than before. The theme amongst a lot of boys seemed to be, *"I'm dangerous, broken, perverted, and an overall awful person that must be kept in the line. The more I act like the girls, the better it is for all of us."*

That, my friend, is NOT a good thing.

Let's get this out of the way early:

You are okay. Really. There's nothing wrong with you.

Yes, like everybody else on the planet, you need to learn how to behave better within our society. That will come with good parenting, good friends, time, and maturity. This may come as a shock to you, but girls also have problems of their own. They have their own flavor of *"stuff that needs to be controlled,"* but you'll notice that people today don't seem to talk about that much, do they? Instead, they seem to be focused on why you, as a boy, suck.

Well, that's bullshit. You don't suck. You're awesome.

Men build. Men create. Men take risks. Men lead. Men protect. Yes, men also go to war with each other. Yes, we make up most of the rapists, murderers, drug dealers, etc. But, if you're like the VAST majority of young guys out there, that ain't you. That's not even close to being you. That will never be you. You're not like that. You're just a good young man trying to deal with this body and brain screaming at you to make babies with young women (more on cruel Mother Nature later in the book).

You'll be okay. In fact, not to brag, but the fact that you're reading this awesomely amazing book means that you'll be MORE than okay. You'll be ahead of the pack. You'll be at the top of the dude pyramid (more on this later, too). You'll be part of the group of guys that just GET IT.

Consequently, you'll be one of the guys that get all the girls. Yes, really. I know that just got your attention, so please try to put away the social media for just a bit. Read just a chapter at a time of this book. Make notes if you want to. Come back to parts of the book again if it didn't quite sink in the first time. If you have any questions, shoot me an email at dso@dadstartingover.com or shoot me a DM on Instagram. Look for Dad Starting Over. I'm happy to help however I can.

Now, let's talk about everything I wish somebody had

told me when I was your age. This is gonna be fun.

CHAPTER 1
PUBERTY

WHAT IS PUBERTY, EXACTLY?

Let's get some of the basics out of the way first. I realize for some of you this may be really elementary stuff, but for others it may help shed some light on a very strange and potentially awkward time in your life. Even if you think you know everything there is to know about sexual development, it probably can't hurt to read through this chapter.

When we talk about all the changes some of you might be going through right now, what we're talking about is a thing called PUBERTY.

If you want to get technical about it, here's how the National Institute of Child Health and Human Development defines puberty:

"Puberty is the time in life when a boy or girl becomes sexually mature. It is a process that usually happens between ages 10 and 14 for girls and ages 12 and 16 for boys. It causes physical changes and affects boys and girls differently."

In boys:

Puberty usually begins with the testicles and penis getting bigger.

Then hair grows in the pubic area and armpits. Muscles grow, the voice deepens, and facial hair develops as puberty continues.

Both boys and girls may get acne. They also usually have a growth spurt (a rapid increase in height) which lasts for about 2 or 3 years. This brings them closer to their adult height, which they reach after puberty.

In other words, it's like somebody somewhere flipped a magical switch that started a series of events in your body that turned you into a man. It's a cool but sometimes scary process.

That switch flip turns on a flood of hormones and other chemical reactions in your body that lead to pretty insane changes. For some guys, the puberty process is a gradual thing you don't notice until somebody sees you at the family picnic and says, *"Wow... you've gotten so big!"*

For other guys, though, it's a not-so-nice experience.

PUBERTY CAN BE AN EXTREMELY AWKWARD TIME IN YOUR LIFE

When I look at old photo albums filled with my childhood pictures, I can tell you exactly when puberty hit me. WOW, I was a weird-looking kid. I got the occasional cystic acne on my forehead. I had big bloody zits on my upper back. I had hair starting to sprout in weird places. I had puffy nipples (a common condition, don't freak out if you have this). My legs didn't seem to fit in with the rest of my body. Things were all out of proportion. Again, I was a goofy mess.

Trust me, girls were NOT looking at me during this time in my life. I had all the confidence of a nervous chihuahua. I was an anxious kid. I knew I looked weird, and all of my actions just made me seem weirder.

If you can relate to any of this... don't freak out. Yes, Mother Nature can be a bit cruel at times, but this puberty stuff perfectly illustrates many aspects of life.

Just be patient.

Not all of us go through puberty the same way at the same rate. Your buddy may look like a full-fledged man, and you may still look eleven years old. That's okay. Just roll with it. You're alive, and you're healthy, right? That's more than what some people can say. Just be aware that this will all smooth out in the end, and you will soon look like a typical young adult man. Trust me.

PUBERTY CAN REALLY MESS WITH YOUR HEAD

For some kids, that switch flip, and the hormonal rush during puberty, makes them feel very anxious, confused, angry, impatient, and sometimes depressed. If you feel like you need some help with all of this, or that you are at the end of your rope and all hope is lost, then PLEASE do yourself a big favor and talk to somebody. Anybody. Your parent, that one teacher you like, that assistant basketball coach that is nice to you, that janitor that always fist bumps you in the hallway… anybody. They are all there to help you. What you don't want to do is let those really low depressed feelings grow and grow and lead you down a very dark path. Some kids during this point in their lives do very stupid things and hurt themselves over what they later learn is a temporary and understandable condition. It was a huge deal to them at the time, but not such a big deal later.

Don't feel bad or embarrassed about getting help with this transition in your life. Becoming a man can be tough. Hell, life itself can be tough at any age. We ALL need help from time to time. I run an international men's group with hundreds of members. We all get together and talk online, have live Zoom meetings, and meet in person… all because they admit they need a little help from time to time. There's not a damn thing wrong with that.

I promise you, a lot of people have been in your shoes, and they'll be more than happy to talk to you about it. This whole *"becoming a man"* thing is new to you. Of course, it's a little scary at times! Not a big deal, my man. You're a dude.

We help each other out. Welcome to the brotherhood.

PUBERTY HITS GIRLS FIRST

As I stated earlier, girls tend to start the puberty process earlier than boys do. You may have noticed this already (like the sudden appearance of giant boobs on some of your female classmates). It's funny what I see when I sit in the parking lot waiting for my kids to get out of school. The differences between the boys and girls I see are hilarious. It sometimes looks like college girls hanging out with a bunch of ten-year-olds. I'm not sure why Mother Nature does this to kids, but she does. It takes a while for a lot of the boys to catch up to the girls in sexual development. That's just the way it is.

Again, this is temporary. Not a big deal. Just roll with the punches.

One thing that we know is that the mental aspect of puberty tends to hit girls harder than it does boys. This is not downplaying what we guys go through, but anxiety and depression are way more common in females, and especially in girls going through puberty. The process of turning into a little woman who is suddenly capable of creating a baby is a HUGE mind F for girls. Menstruation (having your monthly period) is a big freaking deal. One day she was a little girl watching *"Frozen"* for the hundredth time; the next day she's cramping and bleeding and feeling like she's about to die.

You and I, as guys, can't understand the hormonal

fluctuations that these poor girls go through. So, if you have a girl that you're close to and you see her going through some hard times, or you notice that she's going over the line with things such as self-harm (like cutting herself), then let somebody know. She may need some help, too.

PUBERTY IS, IN FACT, NATURE'S WAY OF SAYING, *"LET'S GET YOU READY TO MAKE SOME BABIES!"*

Yes, really. Even at your relatively young age, Mother Nature wants you to go out and make more little humans. Yes, I know... it's crazy to think about that as even a remote possibility. In today's modern world, making babies is an understandably STUPID thing for you to go do. You do NOT want to be a teenage father. The process of making more little humans should happen, if at all, WAY later in your life.

But, Mother Nature doesn't care what our modern-day society thinks about teen parents. Mother Nature doesn't care that knocking up some fifteen-year-old would completely ruin your life and the life of the new teen mother. Again, Mother Nature just wants you to make more babies. To ensure you do the job, Mother Nature has started increasing your body's testosterone level and making other chemical changes. These chemicals are there for one reason. They tell your body and brain one thing: *"GO OUT AND BANG CHICKS."*

Okay, so... should you listen to Mother Nature. Should you go have sex with willing girls?

You want my honest opinion about it? Don't do it right

now. Just wait. The girls... they're not going anywhere. Trust me. There are millions of them. All over the world. If you're reading this, you're probably not ready to jump into the deep end of the sex pool just yet. Relax. It's not a race. Most of your friends aren't getting any either. Trust me. Take your time.

"But... if I'm not ready, then why is Mother Nature giving me all these urges to bang everything that moves?!" Mother Nature is stupid. It makes us want to do many things that aren't good for us. That's just what Mother Nature does. The smarter you are, the more you will listen to your rational brain, not your penis.

Over the history of men on this planet, our penises have gotten us into A LOT of trouble. Go sit with your dad and his friends and ask them if they've ever done something stupid because of a girl. After they laugh for a good ten minutes, they will share story after story about the time they listened to their penises instead of their brains... and they really wish they didn't. Some of those things they did were pretty bad, life-altering mistakes they can never take back.

Sorry to get melodramatic, but this stuff is important and dumb mistakes made with your penis can drastically change your life. Trust me. I know from experience.

Again, take your time. You're probably not ready for sex. Just relax and take this time in your life to learn more before you go into the big leagues.

SEX IS PRETTY COMPLICATED – DON'T RUSH INTO IT

You and other teen boys may have the fantasy of running out and doing every slutty teen girl in your neighborhood, but the reality is that there is a lot of mental stuff involved in sex that Hollywood and porn don't tell you about (more on porn later).

You can fall in love with the wrong girl. You can be with the wrong girl that makes you feel REALLY bad about your life. You can get your heart broken. You can catch a disease. You can knock the girl up. These are all VERY real-world experiences and consequences that you are probably not ready for right now. Hell, most ADULT DUDES I know aren't prepared for it! I see a lot of divorced guys who run out and have sex with a bunch of new women, and they come back and say that they should've waited a lot longer before jumping into bed again. Why? Because sex is complicated. It stirs up a lot of thoughts and emotions that many of us just aren't ready for.

Yes, even us men can get emotional and weird about sex.

At this point in your life, you need to worry about getting your math grade up or how to improve your jump shot. You know, normal teen stuff. Leave the awful adult stuff for... you know... adulthood.

But, if you're like some young men I've known over the years, you will try out sex. The opportunity presents itself, you have a more-than-willing partner (this is important), and your body and brain are screaming at you to do it. If you find yourself in that situation and want to do the deed, please use protection in the form of a condom. If you don't know what a condom is, you're definitely not ready for sex. But, if this saves a few of you from getting a life-altering disease or getting your girl pregnant....

A condom is a sheath of latex (or other material) that covers your penis so that none of your semen comes in contact with the girl you're having sex with. Semen, if you don't know (and there's nothing wrong not knowing... we were all ignorant about this stuff at one time) is the stuff that shoots out of your penis when you orgasm, either via sex or masturbation. That's the stuff that makes babies. Semen holds the millions of sperm that all have one job: Fertilize the female's egg and make a baby. So... keep that baby batter away from the girls. Please. Use a condom.

That's your *"please practice safe sex"* speech from me. When I was a kid, AIDS (a very deadly sexually transmitted disease at the time) was a huge scare, and people were throwing condoms around like candy in a parade. I don't think condoms are preached enough to kids these days, so let me be the one to bang that drum loudly.

You're probably not ready for sex, but if you do it anyway... wrap that rascal up. Use a condom. You've been warned!

CHAPTER 2
HOW TO GET GIRLS

OKAY, SO YOU'RE MORE THAN A LITTLE GIRL CRAZY RIGHT NOW

They're all you can think about. Your spontaneous erections are getting a little out of hand. You're not sure if you're necessarily READY for sex, but you know you want to experience life as some pretty girl's boyfriend. You want somebody to text all the time, to go to the movies, go out for food, hang out and watch Netflix with, etc. You, my man, want a girlfriend.

Well, that goes for you and about every other heterosexual young man your age. Yes, you have a lot of competition. The good news is that it's not THAT hard to join the guys on the winning team. It's not hard to rise to the top of your particular Dude Pyramid. Most guys your age (and ANY age, for that matter) REALLY suck at this *"getting girls"* thing.

Here are not-so-nice facts about boys and girls (and adult men and women, for that matter) and the world of relationships.

1. **Girls are picky.** Because of this, a small percentage of boys tend to *"get"* all the girls. You'll notice this in high school, you'll see this in college, and you'll notice this well into adulthood.

2. **Yes, your looks do matter.** Your overall health and appearance are important. Honestly, you don't have to

be anywhere near perfect. You don't have to look like an influencer- Instagram-fitness-model guy. You just have to look like you CARE about your appearance, and you have to look like somebody who can take care of himself in a fight. A manly dude, in other words.

3. **Yes, your mindset matters.** You need to be confident. Charming. Interesting. Funny. Open. Honest. Vulnerable. You need to have a sense of real abundance in life. Scarcity is your enemy.

In this chapter, I'm going to break down the three areas above and why they're so important for young guys like you to learn NOW instead of after your second divorce and you have three young kids to feed.

GIRLS ARE PICKY

Girls tend to find most boys to be pretty gross... or at least in the category of, *"Never ever going to be my boyfriend."*

It's true. Assemble ten random dudes together and present them to a girl… and she will probably find MAYBE two of them worthy of getting to know better. That's it. At most, maybe two. By her estimation, she will look at the ten guys and VERY quickly figure out that eight of them aren't worthy of ever being a boyfriend. Just a quick glimpse of a second or two and, *"NOPE. Not happening."* I'm not making this up, either. We have data to prove this. We can see what all those girls on Tinder and other dating apps think about dudes. It's not pretty. One report released by OkCupid revealed that women on their site found 80% of the men to be *"below average."* That's pretty amazingly terrible stuff the more you think about it. Eighty percent of us... BELOW average?! That doesn't even make mathematical sense!

But, in all honesty, we don't need science to tell us what we already know. Every dude who has ever lived has learned the same thing:

Damn, girls are picky.

Yep, they are. Think about it, though. For thousands and thousands of years, women have been having babies. After so many generations, they've learned one big thing: WHO they pick as the father of their children is HUGELY important. They gotta get just the right person for the job. Ideally, they want the dude who looks the best, is strong, ambitious, makes good money, and many other essential factors. Yes, girls want it all. That's the way it has been and the way it always will be. Don't try to fight it. Don't think of this as a flaw in their brain. In fact, it could be argued that their pickiness keeps us men working harder and harder. We're all trying to win the girls and make babies!

I know you're thinking, *"Uh, dude... I'm a teenager. I don't want to be a dad. I just want to date girls."* Yes, but we're talking about Mother Nature here, remember? The reason all of us go through puberty is to make babies. We DON'T make babies, though, because we know that is a REALLY stupid decision that will ruin our lives as teenagers. That doesn't stop Mother Nature from screaming at girls, *"MAKE SURE HE'S FIT FOR MAKING BABIES AND BEING A DAD."* Therefore, even a simple decision like whether or not to give you her number is based on those same rules and instincts set in stone by stupid Mother Nature over many thousands of years.

So... Mother Nature tells these girls to be SUPER picky. The girls may not want to listen and actively try to go in the other direction. Still, much of the time, they unknow- ingly follow their instincts anyway. Just stop and think about those few guys in your class that seem to have zero problems getting girls. They have more than a few things in common, don't they? Keep that thought in your mind as you read on in this book.

The good news is that you are being compared to all the other dudes in your social group, and MOST of those dudes in your social group are GOD AWFUL pieces of shit. Sorry for the language, but come on. Some of these poor guys are just terrible to look at. Compared to most of these guys, it doesn't take a lot to rise to the top and get girls' attention. The competition is NOT that tough out there.

I'm not just randomly bashing young dudes, either. I've seen the guys my kids hang out with. I've seen the young guys at the mall and my kids' sporting events. It's a circus of misfits with zero ideas about presenting themselves to the world. They're all girl-crazy, but not a single one seems to be doing the things that girls find attractive. In fact, they seem to all be doing the exact opposite.

You'll learn that this continues well past your high school years. Guys, for the most part, are really really dumb when it comes to girls.

But, it's not ALL our fault, is it? I mean, if you've been in any contact with girls at all, you've probably come to one big conclusion:

Girls sure are confusing.

They will SAY one thing, but then you notice that they seem to DO something else entirely.

One of the most commonly reported *"crazy girl"* things is when they say something like, *"I only like sweet nerdy guys,"* but then you see them hanging all over the tough-looking football player at Taco Bell. She'll say, *"You're so awesome. Any girl would be lucky to have a guy like you."...* but then she seems to avoid the topic anytime you ask her out on a date. You may even hear something like, *"I'm not like that. I'm saving myself for marriage."...* but then you find out that she has a great deal of sexual experience.

What the hell is going on here? Are these girls purposely trying to fool us and keep us guessing?

Kinda, yeah.

Part of it is that stupid Mother Nature thing again. The girl might SAY she loves sweet and nerdy guys, but ol' Mother Nature is telling her that she better go for the chiseled-jaw dude who looks like he can kick everyone's ass. He has that particular something that makes many girls go a little crazy (in a good way). The sweet and friendly kid in math class who does homework for all the pretty girls... he's not going to get lucky anytime soon. That's just the way the universe of boys and girls works. Always has been that way, always will be that way.

THE DUDE PYRAMID

You know how I said girls see 80% of the dudes as not being boyfriend-worthy? Another way of illustrating that point is to see all these available young men like you on what I call the *"Dude Pyramid."* Picture a giant pyramid with a tiny little point at the top and a wide base at the bottom. The pyramid illustrates a concept called a *"hierarchy."* I know, this sounds like a social studies lesson, but just try to keep up here. This is important stuff.

A hierarchy is a system for ranking people. It's something that just naturally happens in all aspects of life. For example, if you put ten basketball players together in a gym and have them play together in a game or two, you will quickly notice that one or two of those guys stand above the rest. They're faster, jump higher, and shoot better than everyone else. They are in the top 20%. As far as the *"young basketball player"* hierarchy is concerned, these guys are the best. These guys are at the tippy top of the Basketball Dude Pyramid. They are at the smallest point. Very few guys fit up there at that tiny point of the pyramid. But those few guys sure seem to get most of the points and most of the rebounds.

What's interesting is you will notice this hierarchy/pyramid thing happens EVERYWHERE. I don't care what little activity or group you are involved in; one or two people always rise to the top of the pyramid. It could be sports, it could be a stupid school project, or it could be on the job. Whatever you can think of, there's probably a hierarchy at work, and only a select few rise to the top of the pyramid and get most, if not all, of the rewards.

This pyramid concept is so universal and common that we have a term for it: The Pareto Principle. It's named after some old Italian economist named Vilfredo Pareto. He died back in 1923. He noticed what people now sometimes call the *"80/20"* rule. He saw that 80% of the land in Italy was owned by just 20% of the people. Then he noticed that this 80/20 rule applied to… well… pretty much everything! It was almost like some unspoken universal law of economics.

Whether we're talking about soldiers, plumbers, accountants, basketball players, and yes… even teenage boys… the 80/20 rule seems to always be at play.

A small portion of people get most of the reward, which is usually because they're better and more competent than the rest of us.

So, what exactly IS it about those guys at the top of the Dude Pyramid that seems to make all the girls go crazy? What exactly is it they are better and more competent at? Read on, my man. Now we're getting into the good stuff.

LOOKS MATTER!

When a girl first encounters a boy, whether at school, walking in the mall, or at a sporting event, she first notices what he looks like. After all, she can't read his mind. She can't scan his brain like some kind of futuristic robot. No, she does what every human being in the history of human-kind has done when encountering a member of the opposite sex. She quickly looks him up and down and determines whether or not he is fit for taking their first quick encounter to the next level.

In a matter of seconds, she decides whether or not to stand close to him in hopes that he will notice her (a standard move in the female human mating dance). She may even be bold and say something to him like, *"Hey, what's up?"* Or, she will make the move that most girls do when encountering most boys out in the wild: She will quickly look, determine that he is not worthy of her time, and walk by him as if he doesn't exist.

Whatever direction the girls take their encounter is first determined by one big thing: **What the dude looks like.**

Yes, your looks matter. Putting effort into your appearance isn't just the job of the girl. Boys need to look like they CARE about how they look to the rest of the world. They need to exhibit some masculine traits (traits that signal *"I'm a tough dude!"*). Boys need to put in some damn effort. Why? Because thanks to Mother Nature, girls are hard-wired to look for a hard-working, tough dude who can take care of them and their future babies.

Let's look at the girls for the moment. Let's look at the work they do to get attention from boys.

1. **They will slather on layers of makeup.** They can't let boys see their pimples and other natural, normal imperfections! Boys may think the girls are unhealthy and look at other girls instead.

2. **They spend hours at the hair salon.** After all, pretty hair is one of the first things boys notice. It's a sign of health.

3. **The more looks-conscious girls (the ones that get all the boys… the top of the Girl Pyramid) are very concerned about keeping slim.** Why? Because most men don't find overweight women to be attractive. Girls know this. It's not a huge secret. It's not necessarily *"nice,"* but it's reality.

4. **They dress very feminine and in a way that gets the most attention.** I've seen young high school girls my older boy's age. These girls will wear very short shorts, shirts that expose their belly area, tight yoga pants, etc. All of these outfits, at a very basic and animalistic level, say, *"Look at me! If you're a high-value dude worthy of my attention, I want you to be able to quickly see that I'm worth your time, too. If you're not a high-value dude, please stop looking at me immediately, or I will call the police."* This is not shallow, stupid, or *"slutty"* behavior. It's natural and normal behavior for a young gal discovering her body and exploring her sexuality.

So, these girls are playing the *"Pick me!"* game, whether they know it or not. Sometimes that game leads to terrible things like eating disorders, creepy guys drooling over them and making them feel uncomfortable, or even a pervert grabbing at them. This puberty/sex stuff, like I say, is complicated. Like everything else in life, it has its positives and negatives.

Think of your guy friends. Are any of them putting in real effort towards their appearance? Most of them probably don't. Do any of those guys have real luck with girls? Exactly.

There are some similarities between what boys and girls need to do to look their best, and there are some major differences. Let's break down the three main points, as I see them, that will put your physical appearance above that of most dudes your age.

GET IN SHAPE

You don't have to look like a steroid-taking bodybuilder. You don't have to look like an NFL running back. You don't have to look like Mr. Perfect Fitness Model on Instagram. You just have to look like a guy who can take care of himself and his woman in case things go wrong.

Think of a make-believe scenario where a dude sees his girlfriend being grabbed at and harassed by some pervert weirdo at a party. The boyfriend elbows his way through a crowded party, walks over, picks that creepy guy up by the neck, and tells him to go home before he ends up in the hospital. Well, that boyfriend will have a very happy and horny girl on his hands later that night. On the other hand, the boyfriend who starts shaking and tells his woman that they need to leave to avoid a scene… and later has a panic attack… he's not going to have a girlfriend much longer.

When you envision what the tough dude in this scenario looks like… it's probably *"strong."*

When I say *"strong,"* I mean *"masculine." "Masculine"* is another word for *"manly."* All those things you think of when somebody tells you to imagine a real *"manly"* dude are all *"masculine"* traits. Those traits are pretty universal in nature. By that, I mean that no matter who you ask, where they are in the world, or how much money they may have, women all pretty much describe masculine men in the same way. They are the same characteristics you saw in your mind when you imagined the dude coming to the rescue of his girlfriend at the party.

Let's get this out of the way: There's nothing wrong with being a strong, masculine dude. For some reason, people these days think that being masculine means that you're obviously an evil bully intent on making life difficult for all the weak people around you. You're part of a conspiratorial *"patriarchy"* that is hellbent on destroying women. That's bullshit. A truly masculine dude does just the opposite. A truly masculine dude is a protector. He's the guy who sticks up for his fellow man. He's the guy who sees some poor kid getting picked on and tells the bully that he will personally break every single bone in his body if he doesn't leave the poor kid alone. He's the guy who makes women feel safe.

We need masculine dudes. We need protectors. They tend to get stuff done. I don't just mean when it comes to girls, either. Being a strong, masculine dude will help you in ALL areas of your life. Men and women alike just respect a masculine dude. Respect is everything when it comes to being a dude. Remember that.

HOW DO YOU GET STRONGER AND MORE MASCULINE?

Your body was meant to do physical things. This is why we have sports and other physical activities for you young guys. You need to get that energy out in a productive way. You need to move your body. You need to push yourself. You need to do physical work to tell your muscles, *"You better grow so you can handle all this hard work!"* Your body was designed for this. To do the opposite (sitting around playing video games all day) does all kinds of horrible things to your body. A sedentary kid (sedentary means that he sits and does nothing) will have too much bodyfat, will be at risk for type 2 diabetes, will have hormonal problems, will have issues with his joints... it's just a giant shit show of problems when you don't take care of your body, and the most basic way to take care of yourself is to move and exercise.

When we see a truly masculine dude, one thing sticks out about him. You'll hear people say it out loud sometimes. *"Well, that dude obviously works out."*

LIFTING WEIGHTS

Well, what exactly does *"working out"* mean? The most obvious version of *"working out"* is lifting weights. You go to a gym, pick up heavy things, put them down, and repeat. That's weightlifting. It should be a part of your life from now until the day you die. Seriously. It's just that important for your overall health and well-being and a crucial weapon in the fight to become the best dude you can be.

Now, weightlifting doesn't necessarily mean moving giant amounts of weight. It doesn't mean you must load hundreds of pounds on your back and squat until you puke. Weightlifting means resistance training. It doesn't automatically mean powerlifting or doing all those things you see the guys on YouTube doing. It means activating your muscles by moving objects. That's it. That can mean working in free weights, machines, kettlebells, or resistance bands. There is more than one way to get the job done.

You should lift weights, in my opinion, at least three times per week. That's the very basics of keeping your body in shape. The good news is that if you're a young guy going through puberty, you have A LOT of testosterone going through your body, and testosterone is what helps you build muscle. So, this is the PERFECT time to start hitting the weights and pushing your body to a more masculine state. You'll see results probably quicker than any other time in your life. Once you see those abs and pecs form... it's over. You'll be addicted to lifting like the rest of us gym rats. You'll have to hold yourself back from going to the gym too much (yes, overtraining is a thing).

I'm not wasting time in this book on what to do in the gym and how to do it. There are lots of books and YouTube videos you can watch that tell you what the *"perfect"* program is in the gym. They all have their pros and cons. One quick way to hit the ground running is to get a workout partner, preferably one with a lot of gym experience. Let him show you the ropes. Let him be the one to encourage you to do one more repetition. A good workout partner is worth his weight in gold. Don't have a guy friend in mind to ask about being a workout partner? Go to the gym by yourself. Ask some guys for advice. Ask somebody to *"spot"* you (watch over you and ensure you don't drop a weight on your neck, for example). Eventually, you'll become part of the club, so to speak. You'll find your partner. You'll be pleasantly surprised how nice most gym bros are.

DO DIFFERENT TYPES OF ACTIVITIES

Ideally, you don't want to limit your exercise to just weightlifting. You want to move your body and push yourself in other ways. You want your physical activity to be diverse. Science has shown us that this is best for your overall physical health.

Sports are an obvious solution. You have practice and games that exhaust you and keep you moving. Not only that, you get to be in the presence of other guys that are all there to have fun and help each other out. Don't like the idea of joining a sports team? No big deal. You can do competitive sports that don't involve a team. Things like Jiu Jitsu and wrestling are just you against one opponent. From experience, I can tell you that there is NO better all-around workout than grappling or sparring with somebody. Any kind of combat sport is freakin' exhausting. Ever try to box for several five-minute rounds? Holy crap, you'll be covered in sweat and need a break before the end of round one. Some boxers do that for TWELVE rounds! That's somebody who is in insanely good cardio shape. Those guys tend to look really good, too. Lean and mean.

Some guys really like running. That's one of those sports you really have to be built for. Some guys, like me, just don't have the build for long-distance running. For those that do, they can go for miles and miles. It's an excellent way to push their bodies to their limits and mentally unwind. It's just them, their feet, and the ground below them. That's it.

Lots of time to zone out and think about whatever is on your mind while pumping blood and making your heart stronger.

So, you have football, basketball, baseball, soccer, lacrosse, swimming, bicycling, running, combat sports, track and field, gymnastics, yoga... lots of different ways you can get your body moving and using those muscles that are begging you to be put to work. On top of those activities, you have weightlifting that will target those muscles and put you into the *"strong dude"* territory. Don't like the idea of a gym? You have a body and a floor, right? Drop down and do some pushups, sit-ups, burpees, jumping jacks, hill-climbers... the possibilities are endless. Have fun with it. Push yourself. Make your body your big project.

Doing this kind of work NOW will pay off HUGE later in life. Just trust me. Fit dudes have way better lives than out-of-shape dudes. Thirty-year-old you will thank you for doing the work now. Thirty sounds like a long way away? Yeah, it will be here before you know it. Trust me.

Do the work NOW so that you don't suffer later.

STOP EATING CRAP

You'll often hear guys say, *"Man up."* That term can be used in the wrong way (like telling a guy he can't ever show emotion), but it can also be used in a healthy way. Often it means, *"Show some discipline. Do what you know is the right thing to do. Stop making excuses."* This goes for a lot of different things in your life. One area in your life where you need to man up is your diet: What you shove in your snack hole.

Dude… a lot of you guys eat like total dog shit. Seriously. You live off a steady diet of fast food and whatever is frozen and boxed up in your parents' freezer. For kids who are a little (or very) chubby, it's time to man the F up. You KNOW you shouldn't be eating that crap. You know it's packed with enough calories and chemicals to make an elephant sick. You know you shouldn't eat it, but you do it anyway. I get it, don't get me wrong. That stuff is delicious. But, like much in life, just because it makes you feel good NOW doesn't mean it should become a regular part of your life. A stop by McDonalds on a once-a-month basis isn't going to kill you. Fast food at least once a day every day will, in fact, slowly but surely kill you. You may not see it now, but older you will see it. He'll want to go back to younger you and say, *"Dude… just go home and eat some chicken."*

If you're going to be a very physical young man and participate in a lot of sports and other activities while hitting the gym, you're going to need calories. You may, in fact, be one of those kids that can eat like shit and still look really good (and I'm totally jealous)… but that doesn't mean you should still keep shoving all that garbage in your face.

What you're doing is building habits that will continue throughout your life. You're going to be out of high school before you know it. You may be going to college. If you're like many, your level of physical activity will go way down. You won't be on the football team anymore doing two-a-day practices. You won't be hitting the gym with your buddies four days a week after school. You won't be outside playing basketball for three hours on a Saturday. Instead, you'll be studying. You'll be partying. You'll be hanging out. You may get a part-time job. Your body will be moving A LOT less than what it is now. But… you'll probably continue eating like you always have. Like shit. That's when the dreaded *"Freshman Fifteen"* hits you (this is a reference to the fifteen pounds many new college students gain). You gain weight, and you gain weight FAST. It's not a pretty sight.

If you're like many young dudes, thinking about your life four years from now is not even a blip on your radar. Four years from now might as well be a hundred years, right? So, when guys like me say, *"Eat better so that future you won't be fat, gross, and unhealthy,"* it's not all that impactful right now. Again, I get it. I was the same way as you.

So, let's look at it a different way.

Go to ANY professional athlete and ask them how important a healthy diet is. 100% of the time, they will say it is one of, if not THE most critical part of their daily routine to get strong and stay healthy. Through years and years of trial and error, they know exactly what it takes to keep their human-body machine running at its best. They know what fuel to put in their engine. That fuel consists of:

1. LOTS of water
2. Protein rich foods
3. Vegetables
4. Fruit
5. Healthy grains
6. The occasional sweet treat or *"cheat meal"*

If these athletes, the guys who rely on their bodies for their million-dollar paychecks, think that a healthy diet is so important… doesn't that tell us all something?

"Yeah, but dude. They have to worry about their bodies way more than I do. I'm not going to be an NBA player anytime soon."

You know what you do have in common with the NBA player? You both have a body that you are forced to walk around with. That body will always be your body. You can't swap it out later. You can't turn it in for a new model. What you CAN do is make sure you do all the proper maintenance your body needs. You can make sure your skin looks its best, your digestion runs properly, your joints don't break down, your penis operates properly, your eyeballs work as they should, and you don't turn into a giant fat disaster.

In other words, if you want to be the best dude you can be and continue being that type of dude for MANY years, right NOW is the time to start putting in the habits and doing the needed work.

It's time to man the F up and eat right.

I know most of your friends eat like shit. Yeah, they'll learn their lesson soon. Trust me. It won't be pretty. Probably 90% of the men my age in my little town are overweight. That's not an exaggeration. I see them at the school events and around town. It's not pretty.

Eating right doesn't mean you have to be super strict. You can do some very simple things that will make you a lean, mean fighting machine… instead of a soft bowl of pudding that's afraid to take his shirt off in public:

1. **Get the grilled chicken sandwich instead of the triple cheeseburger at the fast-food place.** Need more protein (because you're working out more)? Eat two of those bad boys.

2. **Skip the fries.** Some places, like Wendy's, offer something like a cup of chili instead. It has beef, beans, and tomato sauce. Way better than deep-fried potato sticks. Or, go for the side salad. Get some fiber in your gut.

3. **When your mom goes to the store for groceries, have her pick you up a rotisserie chicken.** That thing is cheap, tasty as hell, and filled with protein.

4. **Forget the packaged snacks.** Chips, cheese puffs,

pretzels, etc. They're just bad news. You can down a bag of those in no time, and you feel and look like absolute crap afterward. They have enough salt to kill a horse.

5. **Stay away from those giant Starbucks drinks.** You're not a forty-year-old mom whining about her expanding thighs. You're a man. Men don't drink those one thousand-calorie mocha-frappa-carma monstrosities. We drink regular ol' coffee, instead.

6. **Forget the sugar sodas.** Try diet drinks or water instead.

7. **Need something sweet? Yogurt is good.** Get the good high-fat Greek yogurt. They make some that is filled with extra protein. Good stuff. If it doesn't come with fruit, you can add it. It's basically dessert. Good for your gut, too.

8. **Steak is your friend. Enjoy it.** Grill it if you can. Learn how to make a good steak using a cast-iron pan and your oven at home. Google it. It will transform your life (I love steak).

9. **Fish is your friend. Eat a ton of it.** It's good for your heart and joints, too. Eat grilled or pan-fried fish, not the breaded/deep- fried bullshit that comes in a box. You're not seven years old anymore. Put away the fish sticks.

10. **Like carrots? Eat away, my man.** The same goes for celery. Anything in the produce aisle at the grocery store is up for grabs, to be honest. Load up on apples, oranges, ber-

ries, etc. All that stuff is tasty, sweet, and really good for you.

If none of this is really clicking with you, here's a fact that can't be denied: **Eating well will make you look better.** Your body mass, your skin, your hair… everything. Looking better means you will be above all the other guys who look like crap. Looking better than the rest goes a long way toward moving up to the top of the Dude Pyramid. The higher you are on the pyramid, the better your chances of getting girls and improving every other aspect of your life.

Man up. Eat right. Starting today.

DRESS THE PART

This section is going to be short. I'm starting to dip into the world of fashion and *"style,"* two things that wildly change all the time. I could go on social media and see what the latest fashion trends are for young men and put together a snazzy guide for how to look cool, but by the time this book is published, that information will be old and outdated.

"Dressing the part" can be summarized as *"look like you care."* Using some of the urban lingo from my childhood: You want to look *"fresh."* Maybe you purposely want to look like you put zero effort into your appearance and tell the world that, *"I don't give a shit what you think of how I look."* SOME guys can pull that off. Usually, those guys are so cool on their own that their lack of fashion sense is actually a fashion statement in itself. Think of rock stars and the like. They look like goofballs… but they play to a stadium full of screaming girls, and their last YouTube video got one hundred million views.

You're not a rockstar. At least not at this point in your life. You're a young man who makes a statement every time you step out of the house. For most young men I see today, that statement seems to be, *"I know I'll never get a girl anytime soon, so why bother?"* That is not good.

Now is the time in your life to start taking tangible steps to improve your appearance. Hygiene is a must (please shower and use deodorant on a daily basis), but so are the clothes you put on your body. I don't care if you are showing up to work on a minimum wage job, going to school, going to the mall, or hanging out in a parking lot. You want to look like you CARE. Put some thought into it. Do you have a shirt that is way too short because you grew three inches over the summer? The shirt goes in the trash. Get shirts that fit you better. Are your pants showing too much ankle? Ditch the pants. Your shorts have a hole in the crotch that you hope nobody notices? We notice. You notice. Put the shorts in the garbage.

Despite what many online celebrity types may tell you, you don't have to spend a ton of money to look good. You can go to thrift stores, Target, Goodwill, garage sales… lots of places where you can find surprisingly nice stuff for not much money. The key to any clothing is that it fits you well. Having a nice-fitting shirt in the current style shows that you care about how you look. That is a very important message to put out there to the rest of the world. **If they see that you care, they will care more about you.** It's just that simple.

Now, combine an in-shape physique, good health, a good attitude, AND good-looking clothing…? Wow. Dude. You'll write your own ticket in life. The world is your oyster, as they say. You'll have a difficult time keeping up with all the girls that are on your phone.

That's a good problem to have.

GET YOUR HEAD RIGHT!

It's one thing to hit the gym, dress a little nicer, and eat right… it's another thing to take care of what's between your ears: Your brain.

Many men these days, young and old, have some very troublesome thoughts regarding relationships in general and women in particular. You'll have guys that have ZERO luck with girls year after year, but they are still convinced that their way of approaching this relationship game is the only way. A guy like that thinks it's just a matter of everyone else needing to wake up to his way of doing things. If you tell this guy that he should hit the gym, he'll say that, *"It's a waste of time. I'm not some meathead. Women don't care about that."* No mention of the health benefits of weight training, the effect on your confidence, or the fact that guys in the gym get girls WAY more than the guys who sit around all day and get fat. No, because to admit that would hurt his feelings. It's way simpler to just say, *"Nope. Not true,"* and continue doing the same old thing. It's the easy way out.

This kind of thinking is common in many parts of your life. People think they shouldn't have to work so hard, look so nice, be so tough, etc., and yet they don't ever get the results they want out of life. They don't want to deal with the stress and anxiety that being out of their comfort zones brings. It's easier for them to deal with sub-par results in life than it is to deal with the pressure of changing their way of thinking and putting in hard work.

In other words, they are losers.

You're going to run into A LOT of losers in your life-
time. One really annoying thing about losers is that they try
to bring you down to their level. You'll hear people refer to
this as being *"crabs in a bucket."* Picture a big bucket of live
crabs. Crabs are trying like hell to crawl out of the bucket.
As soon as one gets a good grip and pulls his way up, the
crabs below him start to pull him back down. You'll see
many friends trying to pull you down as you do better and
better in life. This is just human nature. It's something you
have to deal with. Unfortunately, that sometimes means
losing some friends. Welcome to being a winner. It's not all
sunshine and rainbows.

One part of becoming a winner and getting your head
right is wiping away all of the crap that has possibly been in
your brain for too long. Even through you're a still young
dude, you probably have some misconceptions or outright
lies in your brain that somebody else probably put in there
(like believing you are a monster because you're a male
human). You may have put those lies in your head yourself… because the truth was too damn hard to face. This is
common.

So, let's dig into the reality of this *"game"* that you are
playing (trying to become a better dude and get girls). As
I've come to learn over the years, when it comes to girls,
guys have been taught a whole lot of horseshit throughout
their lives.

ABUNDANCE

If there's one thing that hurts men, regardless of what stage in life you are in, it's a feeling of scarcity. By *"scarcity,"* I mean the feeling that everything good in life is in really short supply. It's the feeling that you are lucky to possess any small crumb of positivity you can get your hands on. You may feel that you don't really *"deserve"* any more than that. It's a crippling mindset for a young man, so the quicker you can eliminate it from your frame of mind, the better.

Here are some very real-world examples of scarcity in action:

A guy becomes an adult, takes on a really shitty job, and sticks with that really shitty job for forty years because…, *"Hey. I'm lucky to have this job. I could be homeless right now. I hate it, and so does everybody else that works here, but what else am I going to do?"* That guy has a feeling of scarcity when it comes to his prospects for work. He has convinced himself that he has no other options in life.

Another guy hangs out with loser friends all the time. These friends treat him like total crap when they hang out. They all just sit around and get drunk every night. Why hang out with them? *"They're my friends. I've known them since I was a kid. I don't have much else in this town."* The guy has a feeling of scarcity when it comes to guys he can hang out with and call friends.

Another guy has a girlfriend who is really bad news.

Everyone else sees it. He even caught her cheating on him twice. She routinely puts him down in front of other people. Why does he stay with her? *"I mean, we get along fine otherwise. I've never had a girl like her before. I'm lucky she wants to be with a guy like me."* He has a feeling of scarcity when it comes to girlfriends.

The opposite of scarcity is a feeling of abundance. When you experience a sense of abundance, you believe life has A LOT to offer you. You feel like you qualify for and deserve good things in life. You have value. You have worth. Your boss at work does something terrible to you? Well, then you polish up the resume and get a new job. Your friends all act like losers and treat you like crap? Then you go get new friends. Your girlfriend cheats on you and belittles you in front of others? You dump her like a bad habit and return to the dating world with your head held high.

Sit back and watch most men interact with and form relationships with women; you will see scarcity in action. You will see guys overlooking terrible flaws in a girl because, *"Hey… the chick is hot."* In other words, *"I'm lucky to just be around a girl like this! The chances of me meeting another one like her are slim to none."* It's sad, but it's oh so very common.

Having a sense of scarcity in your mind opens you up to ALL kinds of trouble in life. You associate with the wrong types of people. You put yourself in bad situations. You fail to act on your rational brain telling you to run for your life. Instead, you hang around because, *"Hey, I'm lucky just to be here.*" It's a sad reflection of just how little you think of yourself.

Bringing about a sense of abundance in life is one of the most effective and important tools in your mental toolbox. The world treats a man with abundance like a king. People will fight to be in your presence. Opportunities for success, money, and yes… girls… come way easier and way more often to a guy with a sense of real abundance.

Eliminate the evil scarcity from your mind. Realize your worth. See the vast opportunity and wealth of options you have in your life. Don't be infected by all those scarcity zombies around you. They're everywhere, and they just want to bring you down to their level of misery.

DO NOT WORSHIP GIRLS

Worshipping girls is something that A LOT of guys do. Guys at any age do it, not just young guys like you. Some guys worship their women like they are some kind of goddess. They treat the woman like she is a religious idol or statue up high on a pedestal, looking down on the rest of us mortal humans. They will shower the girl with gifts, do work for her, compliment her constantly, give her money, and, yes... take a lot of negative crap from her. Why? Because she is beyond special. She's a girl.

You may have heard the phrase *"putting the pussy on a pedestal."* I didn't make it up. It's been a common phrase for generations. It means that some guys, after they get to know a girl, act as if that girl can do NOTHING wrong. Everything she says and does is amazingly perfect, and nothing you or anybody else can say will change his mind.

These kinds of relationships are very unhealthy and, usually, end horribly.

Hell, sometimes guys start the unhealthy worship process without even KNOWING the girl. The boy will see that pretty girl across the room. His heart flutters. He breaks out in a sweat. He can't stop staring at her. Something about her is just... wow. She has that elusive combination of *"not TOO hot"* (because being too attractive scares away most guys... just ask professional models) and *"she just looks like a really kind and sweet person."* Then he does what many guys in his shoes do: Fantasize. We're not just talking about dreaming about nudity and sex; we're talking about daydreaming that she's his girlfriend. Then his friend says, *"You obviously like her. You should go talk to her."* *"OH NO! No way in hell. Are you crazy?!"* he says. He's already put the poor girl high up on a pedestal, and he wouldn't dare approach her. It's kinda like somebody being nervous about going up and asking their favorite sports star for an autograph. Same vibe.

Worshipping another person is weird. It's creepy. For many girls who see the worshipping firsthand, it's extremely gross behavior. It's a huge turnoff. When you worship somebody like that, you're advertising your scarcity to them and the rest of the world. You're telling everyone you are a very, very needy person. No girl wants a guy who puts so much pressure on them. When a really good, strong, and intelligent girl somehow gets with a guy like this, the first thing she'll say to him is, *"Hey... I appreciate it, but you don't have to do that. I'm fine, really. Just be yourself. Just be normal around me. Please. You're acting really weird."*

These guys are going over the top with their behavior, hoping the girl never leaves them. In their minds, they've been told repeatedly to always be a *"gentleman"* and to *"treat your girl like a queen."* If you do so, everything will go according to plan. She'll be your girlfriend forever and ever. This sounds great on paper, but these guys usually take things too far into cringe territory. Girls can smell their weird neediness a mile away and they stay the hell away from them.

What makes these situations even worse is that these

kind of guys tend to get with some REALLY bad girls that take full advantage of their neediness. The girls drain them of all their time, money, and *"nice guy"* energy. They chew these guys up and spit them out. Then they move on to the next poor dude. The process is repeated again and again. This happens quite a bit, even to adults. Trust me. I talk to these needy worshiping guys on a daily basis. What you're learning now is what they wish they knew when they were a teenager. It would've saved them tens of thousands of dollars and a lot of heartaches.

YES, REALLY BAD-NEWS GIRLS EXIST – LOTS OF THEM

You will probably run into a few terrible girls over the next few years. That's just a fact of life. There are lots of really bad dudes out there, too, right? Hell, when I was a young guy, my babysitter's weirdo brother was found out to have been a SERIAL KILLER. No joke. As a kid, I sometimes hung out with a serial killer, unbeknownst to my parents at the time. I also went to school with drug dealers, child molesters, drug abusers, and violent offenders… all of whom were dudes.

Again… there are lots of bad dudes out there. We all know this.

So, yes, there are bad chicks out there, too. They're not all angels. They're human beings.

It's a numbers game, really. The more your *"value"* as a young dude increases, the more you will attract girls to you… and therefore, the chances of you meeting one of these really bad-news girls go up.

Even if you are careful to practice an abundance mindset and NOT worship girls, you'll still run into girls that are legitimately BAD freakin' news. They're pretty good about hiding their crazy early in the relationship. In fact, they do more than just hide their crazy. They become super-amazing-perfect girlfriends… but only temporarily.

You know that dream you have in your mind of that super- slutty girl who will do anything with you while treating you like you are the king of the world? Well, that girl... she exists. She's out there. She's also probably nuttier than squirrel poop. That's just one of life's little funny quirks when it comes to girls. The crazy ones... well... they're really good in bed, if you know what I mean. They're like real-world porno chicks. They act that way because they are hooking you in. They're like a black widow spider. Once you're lured in and stuck to their web... it's over. Next thing you know, she's surrounding you in a cocoon of her craziness while biting your head off.

LISTEN TO YOUR GUT

If you're like many young guys in contact with a lot of girls, you're going to run into one or two of these bad-news girls in the near future. Probably more. You're going to fall for them (because she treats you so well), and you'll soon discover that... uh oh... this one is bad news. She'll say or do something that will make you stop what you're doing and go, *"Huh?"* That's your man brain saying, *"DUDE. STOP. PAY ATTENTION TO THIS. THIS IS POTENTIALLY REALLY BAD."*

Do not ignore this feeling. Listen to it. Act on it. If a girl says something out of line or does something that totally comes out of left field, say, *"Wait... what was that you just said. Can you repeat it?"* or, *"Hey, why did you do that just now?"* Don't just let it go. Don't let that nagging feeling you have go unanswered. Don't just ignore it because you *"don't want to rock the boat,"* or you *"don't want to cause any drama,"* or you *"don't wanna ruin the vibe."* That feeling and your responses to it are some of the most important skills you will develop as a man. It will help in ALL parts of your life. It will help you with friends, school, work, and most DEFINITELY with girls.

Some people may describe this feeling as, *"That's your gut talking to you."* You'll even hear it called the *"gut instinct."* It means you have a deep-down animalistic feeling that something is wrong with the current situation. It's like your dog suddenly waking up from a nap and sticking his ears straight in the air. Then he starts quietly growling. Then twenty seconds later, there's a knock at your front door. Your dog heard that unexpected visitor at the doorway before you did. He heard the guy pulling up in his car, getting out of the car, and walking to your front door. You didn't hear the guy until he actually rang the doorbell. Your dog's ears are way more sensitive than your human ears.

Your *"gut instinct"* is way better at picking up red flags than your dumb teenage penis-focused brain is. Listen to the gut instinct. It is wise. The gut instinct was formed by thousands of years of men that came before you. Picture all of these ancient old men from your family tree filling up a football stadium. They all yell out at the same time, *"DUDE. STOP. THE CHICK MIGHT BE CRAZY."* Listen to them, my man. If it sounds like I'm going on about this *"gut"* thing a little too long, it's for a reason. I will repeat it again:

Listening to your gut instinct, and ACTING on it, is one of, if not THE most important skill you will develop

as a man.

Sometimes these gut moments aren't so subtle. Sometimes they are downright obvious. Sometimes they are things you can convince yourself are not such a big deal. Besides... none of us are perfect, right?! Well, that's one way of looking at it. That's also one way to get yourself into A LOT of trouble.

When I began writing this book, I asked the guys in my men's group for some ideas for topics. Do you know what one of the most popular topics mentioned was? RED FLAGS. Red flags are those little and not-so-little things that tell you, *"Being in a relationship with this person may be a disaster."*

Why was the topic of red flags mentioned so much by the guys in my group? Because almost all of them are in the group because they entered into a relationship with a woman that was BAD NEWS. When they look back on their years with the woman, they realize they had many warning signs telling them to run for their lives. But, they didn't listen to their gut. Now they're paying the price.

Here are some examples of some red flags that you may notice in your future girlfriends:

1. **She comes from a bad family.** Dad disappeared. Mom is a drunk. Stepdad is abusive. Her brother is in jail. You get the picture.

2. **She drinks. She does drugs.** If she has this problem NOW as a teen, it will only worsen with time.

3. **She has a long line of ex-boyfriends.** She jumps from guy to guy and discards them like used toilet paper... or, each guy saw the red flags and ran away. Either way, it's not good.

4. **She can't seem to stick with anything.** She joins a sports team and then quits when it gets tough. She left that job at McDonalds that she had just started a week ago. She dropped out of a college credit class because it was too hard. People that quit when things get tough are not cut out for relationships of any kind.

5. **She's very impulsive.** She wants to do it if it's fun and exciting. Even if it's obviously unhealthy, she wants to do it. Even if it means hurting other people, she wants to do it. Even if it means putting herself in danger, she wants to do it. Impulsivity is a huge no-no when it comes to girlfriends.

6. **She treats other people like crap.** She was rude to the Applebee's waitress. She was rude to the guy at the gas station. She's rude to her parents. She's rude to your friends. Basically, she's an asshole.

7. **She's always asking you for stuff.** She wants you to buy her stuff. She can't pay her cellphone bill and asks you to pay it. She wants you to take her out to eat several times per week, and she never offers to pay.

Those are just seven quick red flags off the top of my head. I literally typed those out in a matter of minutes. They are just that common. Every guy with any experience with girls will read that list and nod in agreement. *"Yep, I've seen that before."* Some of you reading this list will say, *"Well, duh... why would any guy put up with any of that? That would be stupid."* You just wait.

You'll meet some fantastic pretty little thing that will make you feel like a god. You will feel better than you've ever felt in your life. Being with this girl will feel like you are taking every feel-good drug mankind has ever made all at once. Then your gut will say, *"Uh oh."* You'll quickly ignore your gut because you want more of your drug. Then your gut says, *"Dude... wake up."* You'll ignore it. Then your friend says, *"Dude... she's bad news."* Time to get a new friend! He's getting in the way of your drug! Then your mom says she's worried about you after meeting your new girlfriend. Welp, I guess mom is an asshole then! She just doesn't understand! Your new girlfriend is perfect for you. She's the best match imaginable because... she feels so good to be with! She wouldn't feel so good if she wasn't perfect, right?!

Just like with drugs, there's always a price to pay. You may not pay the price right now, but you will eventually. It's inevitable. You'll wake up in the hospital surrounded by family, all looking at you with tears in their eyes as they hear the doctor tell you that you overdosed on heroin and almost died. They'll put you in a program, and eventually, you'll get clean and sober. But, there's always that itch to go back to the world of drugs. While you were in that world, it felt amazing.

Drug addiction is the perfect analogy for getting involved with a bad-news chick. Like with drugs, the best course of action is to never start in the first place. Somebody hands you something at a party and tells you it's amazing, and you should take some. You say, *"No thanks. I'm good."* If you see red flags with your new girlfriend, you should say, *"I don't think this is gonna work out for me. Sorry,"* and go hang out with your friends instead.

"BUT, IT'S NOT HER FAULT!"

When I tell grown men that they need to leave their drug-addicted, depressed, abusive, cheating wives, the reply I often get is something along the lines of, *"Yeah... but this isn't all her fault. She just had a bad childhood. That's why she acts like this. I can't just leave her because of stuff that happened to her when she was a kid. What kind of asshole would I be if I left her like that? Everybody in her life has left her. I don't want to be like them. I married her to stick by her through everything."*

You may, at some point, say the same thing about your new girlfriend. Maybe she has a crappy family, dozens of ex-boyfriends, used to drink a lot, used to take drugs, has self-harm scars all over her body, etc... but now she's a new person! She deserves another chance in life! Sure... I get it. But you don't have to be that guy that takes that chance. She's LITERALLY one of a million girls in the world that would be a girlfriend to you. Let some other dudes worry about all of her red flags. You're way too young, and life is way too short, for you to worry about all that crazy bullshit. Seriously. You should love yourself too much to deal with all that nonsense.

Remember… **abundance.**

Let's look at it this way. I used to work for a big company in a big building in the downtown area of a major city. At lunchtime every day, I would walk outside to go to one of the food trucks to eat some lunch. Every day, I would have to walk by one particularly loud and crazy homeless guy. I just wanted to get some chicken kabob, and this guy is yelling out random things about paper towels and George Bush. Poor guy. At one time, that was somebody's baby. Somebody's brother. Maybe even somebody's dad. You have to be some kind of monster to not see that is a real human being who just got shit on by life.

Obviously, mental illness and many bad left-turns in life led him to that spot by the food trucks. I'm sure that not everything that happened to him was his fault. He didn't ask for the schizophrenia he's probably experiencing. He didn't ask for the drug-addict mom that he may have had. He didn't ask to be abandoned by his dad. He didn't ask to be fired from his job twenty years ago (I'm making all of this up, but it's probably not far off the mark). Being a crazy homeless dude is not what he planned for, and it's not all his fault.

So, do I, as a *"normal"* dude, go to him and offer him a

job? Do I tell him he can stay at my place while I'm at work? Do I let him have free access to my kitchen, bathroom, and bedroom while I'm gone? Do I go to my boss and suggest we give this crazy homeless dude a position in the company? Of course not! My empathy only goes so far. I have boundaries in my life. I know where to draw the damn line. That is what saves me from a lot of heartaches and keeps crazy out of my life.

BOUNDARIES

The idea of *"boundaries"* is common in the mental health world. If you're a dude that says, *"People always walk all over me and treat me like crap,"* or *"I always hook up with crazy chicks that break my heart. I just want to find a good girl that will stick by me no matter what"*... well, you probably don't have very good boundaries.

So, what in the hell do I mean by *"boundaries"*?

There are actually a few ways you can look at boundaries. The most common form of understanding them is saying, *"The stuff that you will and will not put up with in life. It's where you draw the line with people."* For example, with your guy friends. You make fun of each other as most guy friends do. BUT... you tell them they crossed the line when they made a remark about your disabled brother. You don't tolerate that and you let them know. *"Hey, cut it out. That's not cool. Understand?"* That's a strong dude with good boundaries. You're telling them when they cross the line. You find it offensive, and you love your brother a great deal. They can joke about all the other stuff, but your brother is not fuel for the fire. He's off-limits.

The author Mark Manson has another way of looking at boundaries. He defines boundaries as:

"Healthy Personal Boundaries = Taking responsibility for your own actions and emotions, while NOT taking responsibility for the actions or emotions of others."

Read that second part again: *"... **while NOT taking responsibility for the actions or emotions of others.**"* WOW, that's hugely important. I can't stress enough how you need to hammer that into your head. The trouble and drama that the girls in your life face are not your damn problem. You don't have to fix her problems. Ever. Seriously. Don't jump to her rescue every time she experiences the results of her bad life choices. She's a big girl. Let her learn her lesson. Let her run to mom and dad for help if she needs it, not to the boy she's dating. That's not your damn job.

I repeat: **That's not your damn job.**

A girl goes up to a boy with low boundaries and says, *"Oh man. I was going to go out tonight, but I don't have any money. I had to buy a new phone to replace the one I dropped for the eighty-seventh time. This sucks. I wanted to see that new movie and hit Taco Bell with my friends."* Low-boundary boy says, *"How much do you need? Will $40 be enough? How about I go with you? I can pay for everything."* High-boundary boy looks at her and says, *"Why are you telling me this? Go hit up your dad for allowance or something."*

Here's the kicker: Low-boundary boy will text the girl ninety times after handing her money, and he'll never get a reply. High-boundary boy will have HIS phone blow up with texts from the girl. Why? Because what he did was attractive. He put up a damn boundary. He showed the girl that he doesn't really NEED her, and he's not afraid to call out her bullshit. She was acting like a spoiled brat. Go take that crap to mom and dad.

You may have a girlfriend who tries to be super nice to you. She buys you new shoes because she says your old Jordans look gross. She redid your homework for you because she said your writing was too sloppy. She cleaned up your room for you while you were at basketball practice. She says she does everything for you because she loves you and just wants to help. Actually, what she's doing is telling you that she has very poor boundaries, and she wants to see if you have poor boundaries too. High boundary-boy will say to her, *"Hey, I appreciate the help here... but you're taking things too far. I didn't ask for new shoes, I didn't want you doing my homework, and my room was just fine the way it was. I'll be the one to decide if and when I need new shoes, or my room cleaned. If I get a bad grade for sloppy homework, that's my problem. Cool?"* If she's like many girls with poor boundaries, she will say that you putting your foot down is actually very hurtful to her. She was just trying to show her love for you, and if you can't appreciate that, then you are the one with the problem, not her. If you were a loving person, you would gladly accept her help.

This is a pretty big red flag. Run for your life.

In short, you want to avoid people that point to you and say, *"YOU. It's YOUR job to make ME feel better. You're not making me feel better, so you are responsible for making me feel worse. Why are you hurting me?"* Run far, FAR away from these people. They tend to destroy everyone around them.

Now, with that being said, do YOU often get mad because people aren't acting exactly the way you think they SHOULD be? Your friends aren't doing nice things for you like you do for them? Girls aren't responding to your friendly ways like you think they should? Son... you have poor boundaries. You need to work on that. Your feelings are not their responsibility. If you expect people in your life to treat you a certain way, you tell them. They have every right to agree with you, or they can tell you that you're being a dick. Either way, it's cool. You got it all out in the open. No hurt feelings. That's healthy boundaries.

If you can listen to your gut AND get this boundary stuff straight at an early age. Dude... the sky is the limit for you, my friend. What a great set of tools to have in your mental toolbox. You'll be unstoppable.

VULNERABILITY

You'll hear from a lot of girls and women alike that men just don't *"open up"* enough. They say we're too closed-up. We're not *"vulnerable."* We don't let our guard down. We keep our feelings bottled up. They claim this is a symptom of a bigger problem called *"toxic masculinity."* They say it's the bad part of being a dude.

Well, they're not entirely wrong. But, as far as I can tell, the problem is not that all of us guys just randomly decided that sharing our feelings was a stupid idea. Over generations, we have seen that girls don't really like us and consider us boyfriend material if we are TOO open and emotional with them. Therefore, we sometimes play it safe and don't show any emotion to girls. So, in a way, girls are partially to blame for boys not wanting to share their feelings. If being overly emotional and crying got us into bed with girls, we would be crying non-stop, twenty-four hours per day.

There's a point where a dude goes from being a strong guy with emotions to a weirdo crybaby that no girl wants to be with. How to stop yourself from going into weirdo mode is tough for some guys to figure out. I can tell you that, like everything else, it gets better with time and experience. With maturity, you know when to share and when not to share. You know that women LOVE it when a man is open with his feelings (because that means he's strong enough and trusts her enough to be vulnerable), but they HATE it when a man seems completely helpless and leans on her to help make him feel better.

A guy who cries because his family was all killed in a car accident is not an unattractive guy. He's a normal human. No sane person would think he's weird.

A guy who cries because he got a B on his test is… a little odd. He needs to learn to better deal with a little bit of stress. There are way bigger things in life to cry about.

A guy who cries because his grandma died is perfectly normal. Death is always brutal, and everyone loves grandmas!

A guy who cries on his girlfriend's shoulder for two months straight after his grandma died… is a weirdo. Grandmas die. We grieve and then move on with our lives.

A guy who feels depressed, sad, and just wants somebody to talk to… is normal. Everyone feels that from time to time.

A guy who starts crying because his girlfriend turned him down for sex and then asks for a kiss to make him feel better… he's a future ex-boyfriend! That is very needy behavior. He's displaying toxic scarcity.

Whenever a guy cries or expresses emotion to somebody else, he's being vulnerable. He's letting his guard down. He's saying, *"I trust you."* Think of a dog that rolls over and exposes his belly while you're playing. He's saying he trusts you and knows you're not going to hurt him. If that dog gets into a real fight with a wolf out in the wild, he's not going to roll over. He's going to bare his teeth, hunch his back to look big and mean, and try to scare off the wolf.

I think many of you guys have had a lousy experience exposing your belly to the wrong person. You thought they were a fellow cocker spaniel, but it turned out they were a rabid wolf. You got hurt. So, you said, *"I'm not ever going to be vulnerable again."* The pain you felt was too much, and you don't want to repeat it. That's understandable, but it's not healthy. You need to put yourself out there. You have to learn and get better. Experience teaches you the difference between *"weirdo"* and *"healthy vulnerability."* You learn that some people (girls included) are just mean and terrible people. That's okay. Your sense of confidence and abundance is such that you brush yourself off and get back on the horse. You live another day. Such is life for a dude.

BE MORE SOCIAL

I recognize in myself that I have some strong *"introvert"* characteristics. Introvert means that I don't have an outgoing personality. The opposite of an introvert is an extrovert. Think of the guy walking into a crowded elevator and instantly talking to everyone. *"Are y'all having a good day today?! Love those sunglasses, my man! What brand are those? Hey, you look familiar. Have we met before?!"* That guy is an extrovert. We've all met that dude.

While I enjoy hanging out with friends and being at parties, I also REALLY enjoy my time alone. If you gave me a choice between walking into a large group setting with a bunch of people I don't know… versus me sitting at home and working on my next book, I'll pick the book every time. But I know this part of my personality I need to work on. If I were more outgoing and social, I would be considered a more attractive dude. So, putting myself out there and socializing more is something that I have to actively work on. I push myself to do it.

Over the years, I've learned that there's actually a part of socializing that I'm really good at. Put me in a room with a bunch of people, and I'll probably leave with one or two new best friends. Why? Because I enjoy long and personal conversations. I hate dumb small talk (you know, stuff about the weather, my job… all the crap you say because you don't know what else to say), but I love deep conversations. I've sat next to people at a party, and by the time I'm done, I know everything there is to know about them. Sometimes, as my wife points out, I gravitate towards the prettiest lady in the room and will get pretty friendly with her! I'm not trying to hit on her: I just enjoy her company and getting to know her. I've learned that I'm a bit of a flirt! I can actually be charming if I want to.

I think part of my success as a *"charming"* dude is that I don't have ulterior motives when talking to people. *"Ulterior motives"* means I have some little secret plan I'm not sharing with the other person. I'm not being charming and friendly with a pretty woman because I want to get in her pants. I'm charming and friendly because I genuinely enjoy her company and learning more about her. That comes across in the way I present myself to people, and therefore they open up to me. They feel safe.

You need to be more open and social with people, especially those you don't know. If being in a giant group setting makes you nervous, that's pretty common. That's a form of what we call *"social anxiety."* Most people have some form of that. One common form would be standing in front of a room of people giving a speech. Everyone is staring at you. Judging you. Listening to your every word. Some people claim that this is their biggest fear in life… even more than their fear of death!

Do you know how you overcome fears and anxieties? You face them. Repeatedly. These things don't get easier; you just get stronger. The people in the room still stare at you and judge you, but eventually, you don't care. Hell, you've been staring and judging them, too. It's just what people do.

Who gives a shit? You go up and say, *"hi"* to them, anyway. What's the worst that can happen?

That's a phrase you need to practice asking yourself over and over again:

"What is the worst that can happen?"

Yes, a more social and outgoing person is usually more attractive. He's showing his confidence. He's actually showing his vulnerability. He's putting himself out there. He's not worried about being judged. He doesn't care about that kind of stuff. All he cares about is going into a room, showing his positive nature, and sharing that with the group. That's it. He had a good day, he feels some positive vibes, and dammit… he's going to share it. That is pretty damn attractive.

This social game is all about how you make others FEEL. A guy obviously nervous or angry about being dragged to a party is not attractive. Immediately, his body language says, *"Stay away from me."* How does that make others feel? They feel uncomfortable. Their body picks up on his signals, and their instinct is to stay the hell away from him. They may attempt a conversation, but his obvious lack of interest in social interaction is a giant turnoff.

Whether you're talking to a man or a woman, being a socially awkward, nervous, and negative dude is not a good thing. It just makes people feel uneasy.

If you feel like you need some work in this area, now is

the time to start. Put yourself out there. Talk more to people you don't usually talk to. Go to the school dance. Go to the party. Get to know people. Ask questions. Be a genuinely curious dude. Work on your humor. Lighten up. Go with the flow. With practice, you will get better.

NICE GUYS FINISH LAST

You may have heard this phrase a time or two. Some think it means, *"If I am a kind and sweet guy, I will lose at life."* Well, that's kind of right… but mostly wrong.

Yes, we have all noticed that jerks and assholes seem to have no problems getting girls. They may also be the ones to excel in sports. Later, they may be the guy to get the big promotion at work. Why is that? Is it true that the jerks and assholes get ahead in life? If they do get ahead, then WHY? Why does the world seem to reward these people?

No, your eyes don't deceive you. Yes, jerks and assholes can get ahead of us in certain aspects of life. The reason, though, is NOT because they are being a dickhead. No, the reason is because of some other attributes that accompany their asshole personality.

Confidence. Assholes tend to be pretty confident dudes… or at least that's how they present themselves to the world. Confidence is very attractive. Their confidence puts others at ease. The girl feels safer with the confident guy. The coach feels like he can trust the confident guy to lead the team to victory. The boss feels he can trust the confident guy with the big multi-million-dollar project. Whether or not the guy is also a raging jerk doesn't enter into the equation. That's secondary to the fact that he is trusted to get stuff done. People can count on him.

Assertiveness. This one goes along with confidence.

When you see somebody who doesn't overthink something and he just goes for it, that guy is assertive. He doesn't hesitate. He's forceful. Think of a guy in a crowded room. People are standing shoulder-to-shoulder. He needs to get to the other side of the room. A timid person who is NOT assertive will quietly tap on people's shoulders and say, *"Ummm… excuse me. Sorry. I need to get through, please. Thanks. Sorry. I'm sorry. Excuse me. Ummm… sir? Excuse me. Thanks."* On the other hand, an assertive person loudly yells, *"NEED TO GET THROUGH. THANK YOU,"* and watches the crowd part like the Red Sea for Moses.

Assertiveness is attractive. It shows that you have low levels of anxiety. You're not a nervous guy. You go for it in life. The assertive guy asks out the prettiest girl in class, tells the coach that he wants the ball at the end of the tied game, and tells the boss that he wants to take on the big project.

Confidence and assertiveness are good things. They don't, by themselves, make you an asshole. Where you go into asshole territory is when you start mistreating others. You treat them with disrespect. Think of the crowded room scenario. The asshole yells for people to get out of the way. As he's pushing through, he says, *"Yeah, that's right. You better move. What are you looking at, nerd?"* The non-asshole, on the other hand, smiles at people as he walks by, and thanks them for moving. He may pat a friend on the back on the way by. *"Hey, Dave! Good to see you, man. Text me sometime."*

I think many socially anxious guys see confidence and

assertiveness in a person and immediately assume that the guy is a jerk. A big reason is because of jealousy. The confident guy has what the anxious guy does not. The difficult but correct thing to do would be to say, *"This guy has something about him that I don't have. He seems to get things that I don't get. I could learn something from him."* The loser way of looking at it is to say, *"What a dick. Of course he gets the girls. Girls just like jerks. I'll never get a girl."* Which way do you think gets real results in life?

A LOT OF "NICE GUYS" ARE ACTUALLY ASSHOLES

Many guys are secretly trying to climb their way to the top of the Dude Pyramid any way they can. Most guys don't want to put in the hard work necessary to rise above the pack, so they try shortcuts. One shortcut is to actually try to *"out-nice"* the other guys. They will befriend girls, do things for them, buy them things, bad-mouth other men… all in an effort to just get attention from girls that they otherwise wouldn't get. Then when they don't get treated like a boyfriend by these girls, they get angry. When they see that the girl likes the confident and assertive guys instead, they get really angry. Some of these guys even resort to violence. They lash out at the world for not rewarding them for their *"nice"* behavior. In reality, they were the asshole all along. None of their actions were genuine *"friend"* behavior. They were trying to get into a girl's pants, and they got caught in the process.

HANG OUT WITH OTHER DUDES

There is something special and unique about hanging out with other dudes. Being around other guys gives you a sense of energy and belonging that you just can't get when hanging out with some girls, or worse, home alone in your room playing video games. Hang around with guys your age now because later in life, it becomes more and more difficult as you get a job and start a family. For some guys, it's damn near impossible as they get older. When those guys get with their friends, they all say the same thing, *I need to do this more often.* Why? Because being around other men is a necessary part of our lives as dudes.

You need a tribe. A squad. A *"gang"* (not a real street gang… you know what I mean). You need dudes you can hang around with and make fun of. Guys you can turn to when things go wrong. Guys who will function as your safety net for when the rest of the world seems hell-bent on making your life difficult.

But why hang around guys? Can't a group of girls give you the same energy and provide the same positive experience? No. They can't. Sorry, I know that sounds sexist, but it's the truth. They can't give that same energy and brotherhood you get with guys. In fact, it could be argued that the energy you get with a group of girls is never TRUE friendship. Why? Because, pull any dude aside and ask him, *"Would you have sex with your female friends here?"* and the guy would reply, *"Hell yes!"* Basically, he's hanging around the girls hoping to one day get in their pants. Ask the girls if they know that the guy wants them sexually, and they will probably say yes, they know he wants them. Would they ever make that guy into a boyfriend? No, probably not. The guy was what we call *"friend-zoned"* a while ago. He was removed from the pool of possible boyfriends. At that point, he's just a *"girlfriend with a penis."* That's not a good place for a boy to be.

Can you truly be a *"friend"* to somebody you want sexually… and the other person knows that you want them sexually… but the other person doesn't deem you worthy of being a boyfriend? Don't you think that would result in a weird relationship? Don't you think that dynamic would get in the way of being real buddies? Most of the time, the girl will leverage this relationship to get things from the boy she can't get from her regular girlfriends. That's not evil… it's just human nature. You don't want to be the guy that finds himself giving girls a ride to the mall, doing their homework for them, or lending them money. Those types of relationships are usually not reciprocal, meaning… you won't get much out of the relationship in return except the privilege of hanging out with girls.

Go hang out with dudes, instead.

DON'T BE INTIMIDATED BY GUYS

Some young guys report that they are intimidated by being around other dudes. They think that guys are sometimes kinda mean. Rough. Bullies. They are not as interesting as girls. I believe that is just their social anxiety talking. Many guys feel like they don't quite belong amongst a group of guys they deem bigger, stronger, and more confident than them. I get it… but that's just a mindset you have to get past. This is a big life lesson here. You need to get over your fears and just go for it. It may mean doing something highly awkward and *"strange"* like going up to a guy you kinda-sorta know and asking if you can hang out with him. What's the worst he can say? *"No, weirdo. Go away."* Okay, at least you tried. There are other guys you can ask. Remember… abundance.

The easiest way to get over this anxiety and enter into a *"tribe"* of dudes is to join a sports team or some other activity with a bunch of guys. That's the shortcut way that most guys enter into a new friend group. My son came home one day after a basketball game and told me about this *"weird"* new kid who just showed up at the game with a uniform on, walked into the locker room, and informed the coach and everyone that he was on the team. The coach had no idea who the kid was. It turns out he just moved to town, signed up at school, and told the office staff that he wanted to play basketball. Unbeknownst to the coach, somebody in charge at the school gave the new kid a uniform and told him to go to the gym at 7:00pm for the game and to introduce himself to the team. They failed to inform the coach a new kid would be showing up. A little bit of an awkward introduction, but you have to hand it to the kid… he had no problem being the weird dude for that one game. He just rolled with the punches, showed up, and had fun.

It took another game and a few practices, and that kid

was officially part of the tribe. My son had him over at the house just the other day. That's how these dude friendships start. That's the way it will be now and throughout your adulthood. I made my group of life-long adult friends because we sat next to each other at work many years ago. We all started on the exact same day. We were a bunch of kids straight out of college starting our real-world careers. We just hung out in the office, at lunch, started making fun of each other, hung out after work, went to each other's houses… and now I consider those guys my best friends in the entire world. We have helped each other out during our best and worst times. We've kept in contact daily even though we all now live several states away from each other.

Us guys are pretty simple and awesome that way.

BE THE TRUE "ALPHA MALE"

You walk into the locker room after gym class and see a smaller, weaker kid getting picked on by some much bigger kid. The smaller kid is obviously scared to death, looking down at his feet and hoping the bully goes away. The bully repeatedly shoves him and calls him *"gay"* and tries to get the little kid to engage in a fight. *"What are you scared of?"* the bully keeps saying over and over. You have no idea what the story is between these two, but this isn't a good thing, and the smaller kid is about to get destroyed by the big goon. He's practically defenseless against him.

What do you do? Be honest.

There is a common phrase amongst dudes on the internet right now: Alpha Male. Some people wrongly think the bully in that situation is the *"alpha."* No. Not at all. That dude is beyond weak. He's so weak and scared that he has to elevate his sense of self-worth by picking on somebody obviously weaker than him. That's sad.

The true alpha male in this situation is the guy who steps up to help out the smaller kid. The hero diffuses the fight by telling the bully to back off because he's about to get kicked out of school for fighting this weaker kid. If trying to play the diplomat doesn't work, the alpha male is not opposed to threatening the bully or actually getting physical with him. He's not about to stand by and watch some weaker kid get pummeled. That's not what a good dude does. A good dude is a protector of his fellow man.

This whole notion of the *"alpha male"* is way overdone and more than a little silly, but I get the need for it. We guys like to try and figure out the formula to being a manly dude. We want to be the one guy in the room who seems to be in charge. We want to be the guy that everyone else looks up to. We want to be the leader. At the very least, we want the respect of our peers. Some people think that the shortcut way to get to this alpha status is to find somebody smaller and destroy them mentally or physically. That's what some people see when they talk about *"toxic masculinity."* They see those small percentage of guys trying to flex their muscles and hurt others. What they don't see is the positive side to masculinity: Helping and elevating your fellow man.

The weaker guy is weaker for a reason: Nobody stepped up and showed him the way to true self-worth. Nobody showed the little wimpy, skinny kid that he needs to walk tall with his head held high, hit the gym, eat a lot more, and make some guy friends. He was never shown that his fellow man is there to help him, not to keep him down. He doesn't see that there is an army of guys out there just waiting to show him the ropes and lead him down a better path.

Be that guy. Be the one to set the trend and stick up for these little guys. Show them what you have learned. Pay it forward, and watch as you slowly but surely become the true *"alpha"* of the pack.

LET'S TALK ABOUT PORN

I know you look at porn. I know you've seen a lot of it. We all know. It's not a secret. I know you've seen some pretty crazy stuff on those sites. I know you probably masturbate quite a bit to internet porn. I know your parents probably didn't say anything about it to you. It's just way too embarrassing and weird to talk to a kid about something like pornography. We hope you go through this phase and come out normal years later.

We old guys also looked at porn when we were your age, believe it or not. Our porn was in the form of magazines like Playboy and Penthouse, or, if we were lucky, in the form of videotapes that our parents or friends' parents had tucked away in their closets. I still remember the first porn video I ever saw. It was at my friend Bryan's house. His mom and stepdad had quite the collection of tapes in their closet (as well as other scary sexual items I won't go into here). They would routinely leave Bryan and me alone at the house, and one of the first things we did was RUN to the closet to find the next tape to watch.

I was absolutely mesmerized by what I saw. Completely naked hot women were doing crazy things to sexually please men… and they seemed to be really into it, too! What's not to like!?

Porn has been around forever. Seriously. Archaeologists routinely find ancient Roman paintings and sculptures depicting people having sex. Dirty movies have been around since the motion picture was invented. Many years ago, somebody came up with a way to record movies onto film. It probably took about ten minutes before somebody said, *"Wait a minute… we could record people having sex!"*

Watching people do the dirty deed is naturally a turn-on. You know what? There's nothing wrong with admitting that. We like to see naked ladies, and we like to see naked ladies doing dirty things with other people. That's just a fact. It's not shameful or *"wrong"* to admit that. You're not a bad person for finding porn to be stimulating or fun to watch.

BUT… like a lot of things that feel really good at the time, there's a negative side to watching porn.

You can watch so much porn that it significantly negatively affects your sexual behavior.

YOU CAN BECOME UNABLE TO FUNCTION SEXUALLY WITH A REAL GIRL

Some guys are so used to masturbating to the *"perfect"* girls on the internet and getting the deed done within minutes or seconds that when they finally do get the opportunity to lie down with a real woman… they can't do it. Either their penis doesn't want to become erect, or they finish in just a few seconds. One of my wife's friends reports that her forty-something-year-old husband can only orgasm if he watches porn and masturbates while they are having sex. This is how they conceived their child. That's just sad. This man and woman's relationship is completely altered because the husband spends too much time in front of his laptop watching other people have sex. It has literally rewired his brain. Do you think that's very attractive to his wife or any other women he may be with in the future (after their probable divorce)? No, it's not attractive. At all. It's beyond creepy.

Porn gives you unrealistic expectations about the act of sex.

Yes, the basics of what you see in porn are real (two or more naked people putting their parts together), but much of what you see in porn is just flat out NOT real. It's an act. It's an exaggerated version of the real thing. Most people watching porn are men, so the porn is engineered to appeal to our basic senses. It shows women who just can't get enough and are willing to do ANYTHING to please the man in the video. They will go so far as to do crazy sex acts in public, allow the man to put his penis wherever he wants, have sex with large groups of people… whatever the porn producers think will keep you coming back for more.

Almost none of this porn stuff happens in real life. Yes, you may get the occasional woman who will do some of those things with you, and it is great at the time, but for the most part, it's just not gonna happen. If you fully expect your first sexual experience to be like what you see in porn, you're going to be sorely disappointed.

Most likely, your first time having sex will be very awkward. It may be the first time for the girl that you're with, as well. If so, then it's REALLY going to be awkward and uncomfortable. For her, it will most likely be physically painful. It's a very big deal for a girl to have sexual intercourse. Many girls report that their first time was a huge physical and emotional struggle that their partner at the time really didn't seem to appreciate or care about at all. The guy's brain was screaming, *"HOLY CRAP! I'M ACTUALLY HAVING SEX!"* The girl is trying to hold back tears and just wanted it to be over with. *"This isn't how I imagined my first time,"* lots of girls will report. *"I wanted it to be something special. He acted like he didn't even care."* The boy was so concerned with doing eighteen different positions and trying to imitate the porn he had watched thousands of times that he forgot he was with a real-life human being who was in pain, very anxious, and downright scared.

Don't be that dude.

PORN CAN MAKE YOU FEEL BAD ABOUT YOUR BODY

While on the topic of unrealistic expectations… let's talk about something we all see and notice in porn: Most people in porn have a particular look. Most of the porn girls have a certain type of body (curvy, in pretty good shape, young), and the guys all seem to have a certain characteristic in common (giant third-leg penises).

It's funny, the guys in porn are seen as dumb, lifeless props. Most of the porn is aimed at guys like you and me, so understandably, most attention is paid to the woman.

Because of this, the guy is seen as a penis with legs. Therefore, the guy is hired for his penis. If you're going to hire a guy for his penis, you're probably going to hire a guy with a big one.

What I'm getting at is this: don't compare yourself to the dudes you see in porn. They are freaks of nature. Ninety-five percent of us don't look like that. The good news is that if you ask most women, they really and honestly don't care about penis size. In fact, most women look at the penises of the guys in porn and say, *"Nope. No way. That looks like it would really hurt."*

So, seriously. Don't worry about your penis size. Certainly, don't compare it to the guys you see in porn… the guys who were literally hired because of their giant hogs.

WHAT YOU SEE IN PORN IS SOMETIMES VERY DEGRADING AND ACTUALLY VIOLENT

Most women do not like to be slapped and choked. Most women don't like being contorted and twisted into weird positions while having large objects shoved into their assholes. Most women don't enjoy being peed on, called a whore, or having their orifices stretched to unnatural dimensions. Yet… you can commonly see all of these things in porn. Yes, some women out there MAY actually enjoy that kind of stuff, and there's nothing wrong with that, necessarily… if they are consenting adults that have openly agreed to do and enjoy this kind of stuff. Those people with those kinds of sexual *"kinks"* are NOT the norm. For MOST women, those things are seen as degrading and terrible acts that they want no part of.

So, why do porn clips seem to enjoy showing these things if it's not so common and most women hate it? Well, it's an illustration of one aspect of porn that is kind of scary.

Many men report that after watching porn for so long, the *"normal"* porn stuff just doesn't have the same effect that it used to. They have to seek out more and more extreme videos to get the job done (have an orgasm while masturbating). In other words, you start out watching naked girls jumping around, then it goes to women having sex with men, then it goes to women having sex with both men and women, and then women with multiple men in a gangbang scenario, then anal sex, then slapping, then choking, etc.

People who make porn realize that the recorded acts need to get more and more extreme to get men to come back to the website to see their ads. That's what it's all about. More clicks and more eyeballs on the screen. As a young man growing up at the beginning of the internet porn phenomenon, I remember how quickly everything in porn seemed to shift to anal sex. It was suddenly all about shoving things into a girl's butt. Was that suddenly a *"normal"* thing most people do in bed? If you were to poll real-life women, the vast majority would tell you that if you tried to shove anything into their butts, they would punch you in the face and never talk to you again. Do some women like it? Sure. But not most. Nowhere near most. But porn sure seems to suggest otherwise, doesn't it?

Again, it's not real. It's a fantasy world.

Do NOT be that asshole jerk guy who uses the girl like your own sex toy and ignores her thoughts and feelings. She's a human being. She's not the two-dimensional girl that you see in porn videos. Those people are actors. They are not real. Porn is not real. Don't use it as your instruction video for how to have sex with a girl… especially a girl experiencing sex for the first time.

Recently, the pop star Billie Eilish opened up about her experience with porn since an early age:

"I think porn is a disgrace. I used to watch a lot of porn, to be honest. I started watching porn when I was, like, 11. I think it really destroyed my brain and I feel incredibly devastated that I was exposed to so much porn. The first few times I, you know, had sex, I was not saying no to things that were not good. It was because I thought that's what I was supposed to be attracted to."

PUT THE PORN AWAY

I'm going to challenge you. No porn, at all, for thirty days. One month, zero porn. Give it a try. Use it as a big game to see how strong you really are. You'll find it's kinda scary how quickly you pick up your phone or start up your laptop to fire up porn when you have a free moment. It's become a habit. Some people may even say that it's an addiction. I think they may have a point.

Zero porn for thirty days doesn't mean zero masturbation. Masturbation is perfectly normal and healthy (as long as it's not interfering with important stuff in your life and you're not intruding upon others). Just don't masturbate to porn. Use your imagination instead. Thinking about that one girl in class is okay and normal. Cranking up your laptop to watch a video of a woman getting a traffic cone shoved into her butt… not so normal.

You'll probably discover that you feel better when you cut porn out of your life. Seriously. You'll probably notice that you have more energy. You may look at girls differently. You may find that you're less anxious. It's weird how much of a drastic effect quitting porn has on guys. Some of my readers and members of my men's group admit to being addicted and then quitting porn. Many of them now feel like entirely new dudes, and they claim they never want to go back to the old them. Sounds a lot like drug or alcohol addiction, doesn't it? Porn… it's not so innocent after all.

BEING A GENTLEMAN

The concept of being a *"gentleman"* is kind of a confusing one. The idea may seem pretty obvious at first, but when you stop and think of exactly what the word *"gentleman"* means and how a real *"gentleman"* is supposed to act, it can get a bit wishy-washy. Some guys take the concept too far into *"act more like a girl because all guys are pigs"* territory. They may think that worshipping a girl and giving her lots of unearned praise and gifts is *"gentleman"* behavior. It turns out that no, that's just needy behavior and a major turn-off to all mentally healthy girls.

When I say, *"be a gentleman,"* I mean to not be an asshole. Be a guy who treats girls well but doesn't necessarily act like a shamed wuss of a guy who just wants everyone to like him. For me, a *"gentleman"* is a guy who doesn't allow his very real and normal human male urge to bang lots of chicks to get in the way of his need to be a decent human being.

To help illustrate my point, here are some tips for what NOT to do:

DO NOT PRESSURE A GIRL INTO DOING SEXUAL ACTS WITH YOU

Don't do it. Ever. If you have to PRESSURE the girl into being sexual with you, then she's not really into it. She's either not ready to take the big leap into the complicated world of sex (which is perfectly ok and understandable), or she's just not interested in doing that stuff with YOU. Either way, pressuring her will, at best, get you doing sexual acts with a girl who just doesn't want to do it. Why would you ever want to do that? Only an asshole with a toxic scarcity mindset would be willing to have sexual relations with an unwilling partner.

You're a gentleman with abundance. You make a move on your girl, and she says *"No"*? No problem! You understand. You're perfectly happy going as far as she feels comfortable going, and you will not shame her or make her feel bad for not being comfortable or 100% ready to do sexual things with you. You hug her, tell her you understand, you're not upset in the least bit, and you both enjoy your movie together. Besides, you have a feeling of abundance in life, remember? You don't put your feelings of personal worth on the shoulders of this one girl. That would be very needy and unattractive of you.

You may REALLY want sex badly with a girl, but if she doesn't… that is not a big deal. It will eventually happen down the line with her or some other girl. Probably a lot of other girls. So why get so upset when one girl tells you NO?

Think of it this way…

Let's play pretend and say you're a guy hanging out with a girl. You LIKE the girl as a friend, but you can't really imagine ever being her boyfriend. Maybe she looks a certain way that you find unattractive. Perhaps she's been your *"buddy"* since you two were little kids and to think of her sexually is just really weird. You might see her as more of a sister.

One day while you're hanging out together, she randomly reaches over and grabs your crotch. Your immediate reaction is, *"Whoa!! WTF are you doing!?"* She laughs and says, *"Oh, come on. You know you want to. Every guy does. It's no big deal."* You then stand up and say, *"Look, I like you. But this is weird to me. I don't like you in that way. I thought you knew that."* Then that girl gets angry, starts crying, throws something across the room, and says, *"All you guys are pigs! Seriously!? Would you like me better if I was ten pounds less and had blond hair?! You're a major dick, you know that!?"* What would your opinion of your friend be now? You would probably think that she's a desperate, strange, needy individual that you probably don't want to hang out with anymore.

Don't be that person.

DON'T SHARE PERSONAL SEXUAL STORIES WITH YOUR FRIENDS

A gentleman keeps his sexual exploits to himself, especially if everyone knows the girl in question. She wouldn't appreciate everyone knowing her personal business, and I don't blame her. What a person does in the privacy of their bedroom (or backseat of your dad's Chevy) is nobody else's business.

The worst version of the oversharing asshole is the guy

who has photos and videos of his girl in sexual situations (like she's naked or in the actual act of sex). Then he shares that with his friends. That is extremely horrible behavior, not to mention ILLEGAL in many ways. It's bad enough that you are violating a girl's privacy and trust by sharing very personal photos and videos of her, but you need to also wake up and realize that this is also considered to be possession and distribution of child pornography.

If you think I'm being a little dramatic here, think again. There are plenty of stories of a girl's angry parents finding out that some dumbass kid is sharing pictures of their underage daughter. Next thing you know, the police are showing up at the boy's house and taking him away for questioning. They access his phone and see all kinds of incriminating text messages, photos, and videos. It's not a good thing.

You don't want a criminal record as a *"sex offender."* That's something that will haunt you for the rest of your life. That's a very real possibility in some of these cases.

DON'T ENCOURAGE STUPID AND DANGEROUS BEHAVIOR JUST BECAUSE YOU'RE HORNY

Suppose a girl you like sends you a nude photo of herself. In that case, you can certainly thank her and say you appreciate the gesture… but then you should tell her that you don't think sending photos like that is a good idea. Reassure her that you think she looks great, but an under-age girl blasting out nude photos over the internet is never good. Ever. It's an excellent way to cause a lot of drama and trouble for everyone involved.

You know how I talked about the *"bad news"* girls that you may run into? Well, one of the most interesting and entertaining things about these so-called *"crazy"* girls is how sexual they can be. Show me a girl who has daddy issues, abandonment issues, a history of sexual abuse, etc.… and I'll show you a girl who is probably sexually promiscuous (that means she does a lot of sexual stuff with a lot of guys). These girls will often get VERY attached to a guy VERY quickly. She will not want to let the guy go. One sure-fire way they have learned to keep a guy around is to provide him easy sex. This *"broken girl"* mating dance often begins with some pretty over-the-top text messages… and quickly goes into the sex acts themselves. These girls will suggest doing sexual things in public, recording her with your phone camera, sending her photos of your penis… all kinds of crazy stuff.

"Crazy" is the appropriate word here. A true gentleman recognizes what is going on with the overly attached and sexual girl and politely backs away. As every guy who has experienced that situation will tell you, the sexual fun you have won't be worth all the awful crazy stuff you will experience with that girl. You have no idea just how bad it can get. Trust me… it can get really scary.

One of the wisest sayings ever passed down to young men:

"Don't stick your dick in crazy."

Listen to your gut. Learn to walk away.

Think with your brain, not with your penis.

A GENTLEMAN = A DUDE WITH ABUNDANCE

So, as you can see, being a gentleman means being a cool dude with a feeling of abundance. It's almost like you are some kind of James Bond character who has been with countless women, battled lots of bad guys, and escaped the clutches of death… all while saving the world. Would THAT guy encourage some teenage girl to send him more nude photos? Would he ask the girl over and over to pleeeeee-ase have sex with him? Would he be so damn needy? No, he would just smirk, tell the girl that she needs to be more careful with what she does over the internet, and then take her out for an awesome evening of dinner and dancing. Then he would drop her at home, give her a kiss, and tell her he will be in touch. THAT guy is a gentleman. He's a straight-up real man in a sea of extremely sad and needy dudes.

A dude like THAT has his phone blow up with endless text messages from girls. Trust me.

CHAPTER 3
THE UGLY TRUTHS

"IT'S NOT FAIR!"

I can't tell you how many times I've heard younger and older men say, *"It's not fair."* These guys have preconceived notions about how the world is supposed to operate. Then they discovered that sometimes the opposite is true… and they can't stop complaining about it.

You'll often hear things like:

"It's not fair: He naturally looks like a model and gets all the girls. He doesn't have to put in any kind of work! The girls just flock to him!"

"It's not fair: I have to go to the gym five days a week just to look normal, and my friend eats nothing but junk food and sits around all day… and he has six-pack abs!"

"It's not fair: My friend never studies, and he gets straight A's. I have to study like crazy just to get B's and C's."

"It's not fair: Just because I'm now looking better and I got a new girlfriend, none of my friends act like they want to hang out with me anymore. I'm still the same dude!"

Dude… life is, to be perfectly honest, just not *"fair."* That's one very true and very negative aspect of the real world. Sometimes, some people get a big boost in life just by being themselves. They were fortunate to be born with their naturally gifted bodies and super-smart brains.

Ask any girl about this whole *"it's not fair"* thing. They are all very familiar with the concept. Do you think a girl who is naturally super-pretty has it easier in life than a girl who is considered below-average in looks? You better believe she does! It is not unusual for a woman to have absolutely everything she needs and wants in life to be provided to her just because she is beautiful. Think of the typical girlfriend of a mega-millionaire movie-star dude. Just because she is pretty, she gets to enjoy the awesome stuff in life that the average gals of the world will never get to enjoy… and they work WAY harder than she does!

You better believe some of the same *"unfair"* advantages exist in the world of dudes, too. Some guys are naturally good-looking, some are naturally stronger, some are tall, and some are born way smarter than the rest of us… Hey, it happens. Such is life.

So what? Good for them! You should be glad to see others excel in life. Who cares if they excel based on good fortune or from hard work? What, must everyone else be miserable for you to feel good about yourself and your life? Be honest. Does it make you feel good to see others doing badly? I would certainly hope not.

I want you to think back on all the times in your life when you stopped and said, *"That's not fair."* How much pouting and whining did it take before the universe corrected itself and made the situation *"fair"* again? Exactly. It doesn't happen. Don't waste time and energy whining and feeling bad because you feel like others don't have to work as hard as you do for the same result. It gets you absolutely nowhere in life.

Instead, you may actually find that there's more going on under the surface than you think. Your friend may be tall and good-looking, but if you really pay attention to how he acts around girls, you may also see that he's pretty confident and charming. It could be argued that his good looks give him all that confidence, but what if you could learn something from him? What if we had the same kind of confidence and swagger that he has, even though you may be six inches shorter than him? Do you think that would help you out in life? Of course, it would!

That's a winner mentality. Winners don't sit around and whine about what's fair and not fair. They're too busy learning and winning to give a shit.

Kevin Hart, the world-renowned comedian, movie star, and multi-millionaire businessman, doesn't sit back and whine about being a really short dude. He doesn't say that his friend and costar Duane Johnson (The Rock) got super lucky in the looks and height department, and that's why he gets all those cool movie parts. No, Kevin made his own path to success on his own terms. His net worth is estimated in the hundreds of millions of dollars. I don't think the words *that's not fair* are in Kevin's vocabulary, do you?

Life is tough. Life is not all sunshine, rainbows, unicorns, and Corgi puppies. Sometimes life just hits you upside the head and then spits on you when you're down. That's just what life does. It tests us. It wants to see what we are made of. So... what are YOU made of?

Here are some of the most common unfair things you will notice as you move along in your journey to becoming a man.

YES, IN A WAY, GIRLS HAVE IT EASIER THAN BOYS

A while back, some guys on the internet decided to do an experiment (this same experiment has been tried by many different guys over the years… always with the same basic result). They created fake online dating profiles for pretty average-looking girls. They wanted to see what life was like for your everyday, not-so-hot gals online. What did they find? Wow… women sure do get A LOT of likes and messages from guys online. WAY more than what your average guy gets. An average-looking girl could just put a picture of herself with a simple bio that says, *"I'm a human female,"* and she will get a lot more incoming messages than the average dude… even an average dude with a very well-thought-out and interesting bio. Why is that? Because she's a girl.

Yes, girls, in some ways, have it easier than us guys when it comes to attracting the opposite sex. I'll often joke that the most boring mom in the world just needs to open her front door and yell out, *"Hey… if anybody wants to have sex with me, you have about five minutes,"* and some dumbass will come running over to her. Probably multiple dudes. If I, your average dad, were to do that, the police would be called, and I would be hauled away to jail.

It's not fair… but that's real life. Your average woman is sought after and highly desired, but your average dude is not. All she has to do is sit there and be available, and chances are that some guy will probably want her on a sexual level. This is why you may go to online dating sites and see an objectively *"average"* looking woman say that she will only date men over six feet tall that make large sums of money. Over the years, her success in dating (easy access to attention and sex) has proven to her that she has a genuine sense of abundance when it comes to dating and the men she chooses to be with. She can, surprisingly, be pretty picky when it comes to dudes.

Do you know what I say to that? Good for her. I'm not one of those guys to kick and scream about the unfairness of the mating game. Why would I complain? I don't want to be with a woman like that. She's not for me. I hope she gets lots of fantastic dates and finds some nugget of happiness in her life… hopefully while not ruining men's lives in the process.

Us men… we can't rise to that level of pickiness without a lot of work and know-how. We must put in the effort to claw our way to the top of the Dude Pyramid. It's not *"fair,"* but it's the truth. Why do you think so many guys fail in life? Because it's tough. Really tough. Some guys just fly blind and have no idea where to start in life. Others have the knowledge in hand (like this book), but they see what kind of effort it takes to win and decide to take the easy route instead. They would rather play video games or watch porn.

I hope that's not you.

GUYS HAVE ADVANTAGES, TOO

It's not all rainbows and sunshine for girls, and it's not all gloom and doom for guys, either. Us dudes have some advantages in this game of life and love.

Have you ever seen a guy who looks gross but has lots of money and power? What kind of women does he surround himself with? Usually, a harem of young and attractive females, right? He and these women have a deal: The girls just stick around, look nice, and give him validation and affection, and in return, he'll provide them with whatever money and stuff they may need. That's a sad and shallow existence and not one that I would personally entertain. Still, it's been real life for many super-wealthy men for generations. We all know it happens. We just accept it. That is the unfair advantage that some super-wealthy men have in life.

Some women have the unfair advantage of their super good- looks, but that doesn't last forever. Ask your mom or grandma if the attention they get from men now differs from when they were younger. Most women admit that they got way more attention when they were the more youthful and prettier versions of themselves. They had lots of dates and received lots of gifts from men. Then they got married and got older… and life, understandably, got a lot tougher.

For men, though, we tend to hit our stride when we are older. Many guys report that their forties and fifties are the prime of their lives. They hit the peak of their careers, they can still stay in good physical shape, and some single middle-aged guys say they can still get some younger and prettier gals to go out with them. If we're slacking in the looks department, we men make up for it with our charm, our personality, our ambition, and yes… even our bank account. Unfortunately, that is not the case for most ladies as they age. It's not fair, but it's true.

Let's also be honest about the big picture here. As men, we kind of rule the planet. Think of the vast majority of the wealthiest businesspeople in the world. They're men. How about the most influential world leaders and politicians? Men. If somebody is behind the scenes controlling this whole crazy world of ours, it's men. We tend to hold positions of power and leadership in the world. We tend to be the ones that take our country into war. We tend to be the ones that determine the economic fortune of the world we live in. We invent things. We perfect things. We fix problems. Men… we're pretty awesome when we put our minds to something. With a lot of hard work, intelligence, and a little luck… we are some awesomely successful human beings.

So, you noticed that young girls tend to get attention, dates, and sex way easier than guys do? Dude… so what? Let it go. We have way bigger things to be proud of.

YOU'RE GOING TO LOSE FRIENDS

I've known a lot of super-successful men in my life. Wealthy men. Businessmen with a great deal of power and influence in their social circles. All of them will say the same thing:

"Along the way, you're going to piss people off. You're going to lose friends. You're going to be the bad guy in somebody's eyes. That's just the way it is in life. <u>If you try to please everyone, you will not be successful in life.</u>" Read that again a few more times. Let it sink in.

You will start winning in life, and that will make some of your friends feel bad. They will say that you have *"changed."* Maybe you have… but probably for the better! If you have a friend that you routinely sit around and play Call of Duty for hours and hours with, but you can't play with him this Saturday because you have to go to the gym and then go on a date with Debbie… your friend may say that you have changed. *"You think you're better than everyone else."* Ouch. It hurts to hear that. You're not trying to be a dick. You're just trying to be a better dude!

They would be your biggest cheerleaders if they were really good friends. They would say that they think all the results of your hard work are pretty cool. They may ask you for advice. They would be interested in learning more about Debbie. A good friend doesn't try to make you feel bad for being a better person. That just means that they have poor self-esteem. That means they will probably try to pull you down the longer you hang around them. Remember… crabs in a bucket.

You have to let them go. That doesn't mean being a jerk and mistreating them. That means saying, *"I'm sorry you feel that way,"* as you keep progressing in life and clawing your way to the top of the Dude Pyramid.

The further up the Pyramid you go, the more friends you leave down at the bottom. You look down, and they all look up at you, giving you the middle finger. Such is life, my man. This is one of the downsides of being a winner. Some people just flat out hate you, and the reason is that they hate themselves. This is the sad state of life for A LOT of men out there.

SOME GUYS WILL TRY TO SABOTAGE YOUR EFFORTS

There is one very sad phenomenon you will see with some guys that you call *"friend."* They will do things behind your back to make you look bad… all in an effort to make themselves look better. This usually involves a girl. They may pull the girl aside and say, *"Did you know that John was talking about you the other day? He said some bad stuff. I thought you should know. I wouldn't like it if he said that about me. I'm just looking out for you. I like you and consider you a great friend. We should hang out more."* Your friend is lying and stabbing you in the back… because he wants to get in the pants of your girlfriend. Yes, it happens.

When it comes to climbing the Dude Pyramid to get the girls, there is the right way to do it (hard work and know-how), and the wrong way to do it (lying and cheating). When you look at the two paths you can take, the *"lying and cheating"* path looks a hell of a lot easier. Sure, it comes with a hefty price (like everyone finds out you're a lying asshole), but it may also get you the reward of getting the girl. As we know, guys can do some pretty stupid stuff just to get the girl.

This tactic has been going on for generations. Every guy sees some version of it at some point in his life. Girls see this kind of thing ALL the time. Girls tend to not fight or punch their way out of a conflict, but rather use mental tactics to lash out at each other. If a girl really wants to hurt another girl she doesn't like, she will steal her boyfriend. That's the ultimate slap in the face and one that every girl has seen happen, sometimes firsthand.

SHE'S PROBABLY NOT "THE ONE".

Let's say you meet and become the boyfriend to the girl of your dreams. Let's call her Debbie. She's really pretty. She's super smart. She's funny. She likes a lot of the same things that you like. She is your soul mate. If you think about it, how crazy lucky can a dude be?! You found the perfect heavenly girlfriend… all because you happen to be in the same math class as her! What are the chances, right?

Well, the chances are pretty slim that Debbie will be your girl forever and ever. That's just the truth. You are VERY VERY young, and you will both go through massive life changes as you get older. I can speak for all guys out there today when I say:

"I am not the same dude I was when I was a teenager. I am not the same dude as I was in my twenties. Hell, I'm not the same dude I was in my thirties. As I go through life, I learn, win, fail, and win again… and change a great deal along the way. It is VERY tough to find one person that will be along for the ride and stick by you through it all as you navigate all these life changes. It's almost impossible."

A more realistic scenario is that you will date several girls throughout your adult life. You could realistically *"date"* twenty or more women. I know guys who have been with over a hundred girls before deciding on the one woman to call *"wife."* Some guys never walk down the aisle and marry a woman. They stay single for life. You know what? There's nothing wrong with that. The marriage thing isn't for everyone.

If you feel that meeting one girl, getting married, and starting a family is for you… then take your time. Don't settle down with the one girl from your small-town high school math class. Get out. See the world. Travel. Learn. Save money. Build your little personal empire. Get to know lots of different women. Practice dating. Practice being a boyfriend. The more you do it, the better you get at it! Show me a guy who is thirty years old, single, has a lot of money in the bank, owns his own business, has a college degree, is well-traveled, and has dated lots of women from all over the world… and I'll show you a guy who has a much higher chance of making marriage work. He has lots of life skills and wisdom. He knows what is good in life and what isn't. He knows his own personal value. **He has a very real sense of abundance in life.**

That's your goal.

Debbie from math class may be great, but she may also slow you down in life and keep you from realizing your full potential. That's not a slam against Debbie. She may be a wonderful human being. She MAY be the type of girl you want to wife-up later in life… but put that idea on the shelf for another ten or fifteen years. If she truly is THE ONE, she'll be there when you're ready.

I'm speaking on behalf of the millions of men who married their high school sweethearts. Trust me, it felt more than right at the time, but experience showed us that we didn't know what we were doing. We were very young and very inexperienced. Youth and inexperience are two things that can hurt you a great deal in the long-term relationship game.

Just like mortgages, car payments, and arthritis... serious relationships are best left for adulthood.

IT'S TOUGH TO FIND A GIRL WITH VERY FEW RED FLAGS

You know in chapter three how I talked about the *"bad-news"* girls you will run into and how to spot the *"red flags"* when it comes to dating? Well, from what I can tell (and based on what others tell me), the current population of girlfriend candidates has a surprisingly huge number of bad-news girls that have more red flags than a Chinese parade.

In other words, it's now tougher than ever to find a really good girl that will not be a drama-filled nightmare. That's just the sad reality of the girlfriend market today. Why is that? Well, I can think of a variety of reasons. Here are a couple of big ones:

1. **Divorce is terrible… and also terribly common.** Divorce can do some real emotional damage to a kid. Just because a girl comes from a broken home doesn't mean she's bad news, but the chances of her having some real emotional issues went up quite a bit if her mom and dad split up. If you date a girl that ends up being ten kinds of crazy, the chances are pretty high that she didn't have dear ol' dad around very much. The science and statistics prove that the girl's relationship with her father greatly impacts how she navigates relationships with boys. The term *"daddy issues"* exists for a reason.

2. **Thank you, internet.** Right now, any girl on the planet can go on some app like TikTok, upload some videos of her doing a stupid dance in a tiny outfit, and she will be

flooded with instant validation. Thirsty guys from all over the planet will tell her that she is beyond amazing. Some may even send her money. That may sound like a good thing for her self-esteem, but it's actually been proven to be bad for her overall mental health.

I know social media is huge for you guys, but it's not a good thing. It's turning all of you into ADHD kids with zero attention spans and a false sense of what is *"attractive"* in people. Jiggling your butt for millions of strangers while lip-syncing some line from a movie is not cute… it's concerning behavior. I know I sound like an old fart here, but I've seen what TikTok videos consist of. I saw young teen girls wearing thongs, twerking for the camera, lip-syncing to songs, and talking about performing oral sex on guys. All of this is just a giant, loud cry for help.

You and I may be able to laugh at the things we see on social media, but some girls take that stuff VERY seriously and it messes with their sense of self-worth. There is no reason for a sixteen-year-old girl to wear super-tight yoga shorts to show her butt off on TikTok. The only reason is to get likes and views. She has reduced herself to an object that just wants attention. That is not a good thing. I don't care how you frame it. That will not have a good effect on that girl's mental health. It's one thing to explore your sexuality, it's another to do so for the sake of getting validation from millions of strangers all over the world who just want to have sex with you.

This social media stuff can go beyond things like being a stupid sex object. I'm sure you've heard about people *"cutting,"* right? It's when kids (primarily young girls) harm themselves on purpose. They do so out of some super unhealthy desire to *"feel"* something, no matter how harmful it may be. It's a sign of some pretty significant emotional distress. Well, guess why cutting became so popular. Yep, because of social media. One girl shared her story of cutting… then another… then another… and next thing you know, millions of girls are doing it, too. Why? Because it's now socially acceptable. Ninety percent of those girls would've never even conceived of the idea of cutting before seeing something about it on Instagram.

In short, this being a *"mentally troubled teen girl"* stuff is really contagious.

So, if you have a girl who is already more than a little anxious and not sure about her role in life, something like social media can send her into a full-blown depression and other issues that make it very difficult for her to form real healthy relationships with other people. This doesn't apply to everyone, of course, but enough to know that it's a genuine problem that we need to address in a big way.

ALL OF THIS "*WINNING AT LIFE*" STUFF IS DIFFICULT

Exercising regularly.
Eating right.
Keeping your appearance sharp.
Working hard at school.
Being a gentleman.
Working hard at your job.
Keeping your mind straight.
Planning for college.
Thinking about a career.
Dating girls.

None of this is easy. None of it. It's flat-out tough work. It is VERY easy for any of us at any time to say, *"Screw this. I'm going to be lazy."* Life sure does give us many opportunities to just give up and do the wrong thing, doesn't it?

Here are some common scenarios to illustrate my point:

If I'm driving around town and feeling really hungry, I will see twenty fast food restaurants all begging me to pull in and get a number three meal with large fries and a milkshake. In a matter of minutes, I could pull my car over, give some dude nine dollars, and leave with a meal that consists of about eighteen hundred calories. It will feel terrific in the moment, but it will make me gain a couple of pounds and probably give me diarrhea. Or, I could wait for another hour or so until I get home, make some chicken, rice, and a nice fruit salad. But… that sounds like work. Sounds like more time being hungry. It's also the right thing to do.

I tell myself that I will exercise five days per week. I'm coming up on the end of the week, and I've only exercised three times. I had to work a lot on a big project for a class I'm taking, plus my job, plus family time, so I haven't had much free time at the end of the day. I'm exhausted. I just want to lie down. I could be happy with three days of exercise and tell myself I did enough… but I know myself. That would quickly become a bad habit. No, I have to get my butt up, put on my headphones, and go for a long one-hour walk. The next day I will hit the gym. That will give me my five sessions for the week. I will go to bed a little more tired and satisfied, knowing I stuck to my goal. Then I will do it again next week and the week after.

A crazy (but hot) girl I know calls me and asks if I want to hang out. She's bored, there's a new movie she wants to see, and none of her girlfriends can go. I'm bored too, so I say, *"Sure."* We meet at the movies. She starts getting a little handsy and grabby with me. I smell alcohol on her breath. She asks me to go to a nearby bar and restaurant with her. I go. She drinks six beers while we're there. Her speech is slurring. She's getting more grabby as the night goes on. Finally, she leans into me drunkenly and says, *"I'm too drunk to drive. If you take me home now, you can do whatever you want to me. Seriously. I'm horny."* It would be very simple for me to take this drunk girl home and have a good time, but instead, I tell her that I have to be up early the next morning… so I'll have to pass. *"Thanks for the invitation, though!"* I recognize that she probably has a bad drinking problem, and I'm not desperate enough to have sex with somebody like that. I don't need that kind of person in my life. Hanging out with her for one evening is enough.

In each of these pretty realistic scenarios, we're talking about something called discipline. Discipline is doing the right thing when you REALLY don't feel like it. Discipline takes practice. It takes doing the correct-but-difficult thing, again and again, day after day. Eventually, doing the right thing just becomes a habit.

If you study every winner in the history of the world, they are disciplined people. They do important things every single day, no matter what. Any world leader, world-class athlete, successful entertainer, business mogul… all highly disciplined people. They are driven by their need to conquer life and the wisdom to know that many people are willing to take their place.

If you don't go to the gym today as you planned, you better believe some other dude will be going. He will look better than you. He will be happier and healthier. He will put in the one hour of work and do that one hour over and over for months on end. He will be a lean, mean fighting machine. You won't be. People will call him *"lucky"* to be in such good shape. He will laugh at them and continue on doing the work, anyway.

If you go to bed with that crazy drunk girl, you will have to endure the weeks of non-stop crazy text messages. You will have to put up with a crying drunk woman on your doorstep at 2:00am on a Wednesday. You will have to deal with your boss telling you that some *"strange girl"* is asking for you outside in the lobby and won't leave until she talks to you. You will be embarrassed. You will be ashamed. You will eventually have to tell her to leave you alone. That's when the real drama begins. Sometimes the drama gets so bad the police are called to your home, and you are taken away in handcuffs for something you didn't do.

In hindsight, you will tell yourself that you should've had the discipline and strength to say to the girl, *"NO,"* when she asked you to sleep with her. Now you pay the price. Now you're one of the bazillion guys screaming, *"All girls are crazy."* In reality, all you had to do was listen to your gut and avoid the obvious red flags that everyone else saw. You didn't. You thought with your penis and not with your rational brain.

Discipline saves you from a lot of drama and heart-ache.

As you progress through high school and into college, you're going to be presented with A LOT of temptation to skip on the discipline stuff and go right to *"party animal"* mode, or *"fat slob"* mode, or *"hang out and play video games with my bros all day and complain about girls"* mode. Trust me, dude. You'll be confronted with those temptations on a daily basis. I should know. I'm a dude. I went to college.

Thankfully, I was so busy going to class, working, and trying to make money to pay my rent, that I didn't have much time to get into trouble in college. Part of me wishes I had a little more fun, and another part is thankful that I learned early on how far discipline can get me. I would later have plenty of fun in adulthood. I've been all over the world, done some awesome things, and have met amazing people. Here I am now writing another book that thousands of awesome dudes like you will read. I wouldn't be in this spot in life if I didn't have discipline.

DON'T WAIT FOR MOTIVATION

So many people just sit around and wait for some kind of motivation to hit them and light a fire under their butts. You'll hear people stuck in a rut say, *"Man, I just need something to get me going."* This is a really bad mindset to get in. You'll constantly be chasing things that give you a high and reason to move. Newsflash, amigo: Life isn't a series of awesome motivations. Sometimes, life is just dull. Sometimes you look at your calendar for the next two months and say, *"Class... work... gym... that's it?"* Yep, that's it. If you want more out of life, you need to get up and MAKE more out of life. Don't sit and wait for the rest of the world to hand you happiness and meaning on a silver platter. It doesn't work that way.

As the famous author, podcast host, businessman, and former Navy Seal, Jocko Willink famously says, *"Discipline = Freedom."* Do the stuff you need to do now, do it repeatedly no matter what, and the world opens up to you.

CHAPTER 4
CONGRATS, YOU'RE A HIGH-VALUE DUDE

LET ME FILL YOU IN ON THE SECRET...

In case you haven't figured it out yet, there are no tricks to *"get girls."* There's no special subset of actions that are just for the sake of getting girls to like you. The actions that get girls to like you are the same actions that result in an overall more successful life.

To get more girls, you need to be a better man. That's the trick. Be a better overall dude, and your chances of getting girls go WAY up. The girls are just a byproduct of a better life. They are the icing on the cake.

Yes, there are many guys out in the world that will sell you expensive online courses trying to teach you *"game"* and *"pickup artist"* tricks for getting girls to drool over you. These guys are treating women like lab rats. They're sitting back and watching how women act when high-value guys do certain things, and then these men go out and replicate those things in the real world. While the tips and tricks may "work" (these guys get more sex than before), these men are missing the way bigger picture.

What these pickup artist guys are doing is ACTING like high-value dudes. They are doing some of the behaviors that high-value dudes do... without actually being high-value dudes. For example:

You'll often hear guys telling men not to answer a girl's text message right away. Why? Because that gives the appearance of being busy. You have important things to do.

You can't just hang out on your phone all day waiting for the text message from the one girl you met last night. Besides, you may have a bunch of other women you're talking to. You're distracted by bigger and better things. You're acting like a man of status.

Does it work? Sure. But do you know what the best way to pull this off is? To ACTUALLY BE A BUSY MAN WHO HAS MORE IMPORTANT THINGS TO DO THAN STARE AT HIS PHONE ALL DAY. An actual man of status is busy working, learning, going out and meeting people… you know, high-value-dude stuff. Do you know what he doesn't do? Sit on his butt and stare at his phone like a bored housewife.

Sure, a case could be made that you should *fake it 'til you make it,* but I don't think that necessarily applies here. What, you're going to fake being busy until… when, exactly? The true answer is: You fake it until you snag the girl and get her into bed. Okay… and then what? Continue faking it until she gets tired of you and figures out you're fake? Really? That's your plan?

You're still going to be you. You're still the low-status guy pretending to be something you are not. You are still playing a role. You're an actor. Eventually, people will see through the act and treat you like a pariah (another word for a social outcast… a guy nobody wants anything to do with).

People, women included, tend to be drawn to genuine people. "But, women are picky and want genuinely high-value dudes." Yep, so you better get to work if you want to join the club of men that are successful with life and women. There are no shortcuts in life… and therefore, there are no shortcuts in this whole relationship game.

The key to getting girls? Be a high-value dude. How do you get to be a high-value dude? Hard work and know-how. I've given you the knowledge, now you just need to do something with it.

ONE THING AT A TIME

For young and old men alike, taking inventory of all the things you need to *"fix"* in your life can be a little overwhelming. Fitness, attitude, diet, etc., it's too much! Well, if that's how you feel right now, then just tackle ONE thing. After you have successfully laid out a plan for that one thing, you can move on to the next thing.

For many guys that I work with, that first step is usually the fitness route. A LOT of dads out there, in case you didn't notice, are really out of shape. They completely neglect their physical bodies, and it shows. Their wives lose attraction to them, they are embarrassed to take their shirts off, their kids make fun of them… it's not pretty. THEN they lose weight and gain some muscle. They look better. They feel more confident. People respect them more. They get more sex from their wives. Now they have a real foundation to build on. Their newfound confidence allows them to tackle the really hard stuff, like trying to face all the drama from their childhood.

I think you can learn from all of those older guys and make sure you have the foundation of your body and fitness squared away. It's absolutely amazing how much that can change a young man. I remember when I was a kid on the high school basketball team. I wasn't good at basketball (okay, I was terrible), but I was good at the pre-season weightlifting. My body just took off. I gained muscle I didn't know I had! It was awesome. That started a lifelong habit of fitness that has continued, in some form, for thirty years.

What's interesting is that my life took a major downturn when I stopped working out. Without that foundation, everything crumbled. I didn't realize just how important that was for my overall mental and physical health. I think every other dude who dragged his butt back into the gym will tell you the same thing: Get your body right, and the rest tends to follow.

Okay, so you're already in good shape. You exercise often. Now what? Well, it's time to work on the mental stuff. Go back to chapter two, part three - *"Get Your Head Right."* Work on one thing at a time. Step back and really take an honest look at yourself. Do you really have a genuine sense of *"abundance"* in life? Are you treating girls like a queen just because they are girls? How about your boundaries? Did you stop porn yet? Lots of things to work on!

Treat this whole thing like a big game. YOU are in control, my man. Not your school, not your parents… YOU. That should be exciting. That should fill you with a sense of energy, not a sense of being overwhelmed. You take things at the speed you feel comfortable with. Rome wasn't built in a day. This stuff takes time and effort to do it right. The good news is that you are young. Holy shitballs, my man. You have your whole life ahead of you. Your roadmap is empty. YOU are designing the map as you go along. Nothing says that you can't erase the path and go back and start over. Do that as many times as you want.

What makes this even more exciting is that you are

NOT ALONE. You have an army of dudes all doing the same damn thing. Make sure that you surround yourself with the right people. You want winners on your side. You want people with a positive attitude. You want people who support you. You want people who tell you when you're doing the right thing, and when you're going down the wrong path. You want a tribe. A team. Get out there and make lifelong friends that will assist you along the way. Be the guy who steps up to help others in need.

If you combine the proper physicality, the mindset, AND a tribe of winners around you… Dude. I'm not exaggerating when I say that I get goosebumps just thinking about the possibilities for a young man like you. Some of you reading this are literally at the beginning stages of life that most of us only see in movies. Somebody will later study your life looking for answers. They will want to know your secret. Some will claim that you are just *"lucky."* That's horseshit, of course. The irony is that they know it's horseshit. But, the reality is too tough for them to see. They had the same damn tools that you have. The knowledge was always there. They were just too damn busy doing the wrong things. They didn't pay attention. Life is now biting them in their asses.

Damn, dude. I wish I had this book when I was your age. To be honest, I saw this wisdom all around me as a kid on a daily basis. I just didn't pay attention. I didn't act on it. Nobody put this stuff together for me in a convenient book like this. Instead, it was presented in the form of little life lessons repeated again and again. When did I listen? Oh, around my mid-thirties… when my first wife left me and turned my world upside-down. To be honest, I should buy her a big thank you gift. That was the giant wakeup call that I needed. It took a great deal of pain to wake my dumbass up. You, thankfully, don't have to experience that same level of pain.

Think of this book as the father figure putting his arm around you saying, *"Look, kid. Let me save you a few decades of a rough life and tell you how to do things the right way."* Then you look behind you and see a giant ocean of more dads, brothers, and friends all ready to help you, too.

You're not alone. You never will be. Take this knowledge and DO something with it. The world is waiting for you to make your mark.

That's REAL TALK, my man. I wouldn't bullshit you.

FREQUENTLY ASKED QUESTIONS

Here are some common questions that I hear from men, young and old. Do you have a question? Shoot me an email at dso@dadstartingover.com.

My friends are having sex. I would say that they are mostly having sex with what you would call "bad news" girls. They are seeing a lot of drama and it can get crazy… but, they're having sex and I'm not. I'm noticing more opportunities to have sex, and I feel like I want to do it. It's hard to pass up.

Yes, and they are setting up a pattern of behavior that will cause them A LOT of harm in the future. They are having success at having sex with crazy chicks. Well, congrats. Check in with that guy again at age thirty and see how his life is, versus the guy who was picky about who he spent his time with. The dude with the crazy chicks will only know how to interact successfully with crazy chicks, and he will wonder why his life is so awful and full of drama.

Maybe you can enjoy time with these girls, and it won't affect you in that way, now or in the future. Just be aware that as far as *"drugs"* are concerned, there is nothing quite as addictive as a *"crazy"* girl who will do anything in bed. We all know how stories of drug use end. Be careful.

All of the girls that I know are sending out nude photos of themselves to guys they like. I know it's not "right", but if I wait until I find the "right" girl, I'm afraid I will never have sex. I don't want to wait for some boring super-religious girl who will end up being terrible at sex. I actually want to have sex with lots of girls and have fun in life. Waiting for the perfect girl sounds boring.

Nobody says you have to wait for Ms. Perfect. Sure, have fun, but just be aware of what you might be getting yourself into. I know sending nude photos is a common trend these days, but it doesn't make it right. If these girls are under eighteen years of age, you need to be VERY careful. All it takes is ONE girl to run to parents or police, and oh boy is your world about to change. Just cover your butt and let the girls know they don't have to do that. You'd prefer to see the real thing one day, and you can wait.

I've always been very small and I've been bullied off and on my whole life. I'm almost done with high school, and the idea of going into college is kind of scary. I don't want to end up being bullied all over again and have to endure four more years of hell. I'm not sure how to start college off so I can do things the right way.

Sorry you had to go through that period of your life, my man. The good news is that you are turning the page on that chapter and now you can be whoever the hell you want to be. Hit the gym. Hit the cafeteria. Hit on girls. Now is the time for a total transformation. Make a new friend group. You'll find a lot more diverse population of students in college. Have the time of your life. Remember: ABUNDANCE.

My mom and dad divorced. I live mostly with my mom.

She spends most of her time telling me to be a sweet, nice guy, and not like my dad. She's telling me that most of the girls out there aren't good enough for me and I should wait until I'm much older to date. I'm confused.

I can't tell you how many older guys I talked to were raised in the exact same scenario. They all ended up being very codependent in nature (Google the term). You may want to read a book called *"No More Mr. Nice Guy"* by Dr. Robert Glover. It will probably open your eyes to just how unhealthy this relationship with mom can be. You're not mom's little husband. You're an independent dude who needs to go out and experience life. Your mom is probably trying her best to raise a son, but she's going about it the wrong way.

I feel pressured to have sex. I really don't think I'm ready, but I have friends telling me that you just have to do it once and get it over with. They've all done it and they seem to have changed a lot. I'm a shy guy and always have been. I've had opportunities to have sex, but just couldn't do it. Do I need to man up and do the deed?

It's not a race. Do it when you feel ready. There is PLEN-TY of other stuff you can work on prior to doing the dirty deed with a girl. Work on your fitness, your social skills, your schoolwork, sports, flirting with girls, etc. You're trying to jump from step A to step Z. There's a lot in between.

My girlfriend and I have been together for three years. My family and her family are both asking if we have

One negative part of life in the relationship game: You're going to break hearts. Your mind and heart aren't in it, she's assuming some pretty big things about the two of you, and you feel some unnecessary pressure from everyone to take things further. Will you find somebody else as good as her? Of course. Abundance, my man. Your gut is telling you something is off, and you have a mission to go out and experience life as a bachelor. Speaking on her behalf, she wants to be with a guy who is just as crazy about a future with her as she is with him. That doesn't sound like it is you. Let her go so she can find that guy.